Merry Christmas '97

Les,
Stephen & Kate

Page 117
House where I
Lived with MOMA +
PoppA Stone until I
was 7 years old.
Pop was Farm Boss for
Green's for 21 years.
Dwight Sarver

A Kentucky Family Biography
1795 - 1965

THE GREENS OF FALLS OF ROUGH

by

HUGH A. RIDENOUR

McClanahan
Publishing House

Cover design and book layout by James Asher Graphics
Back cover art courtesy of Maglinger Corp., Owensboro, Kentucky

Manufactured in the United States of America

All book order correspondence should be addressed to:

Treetops Enterprises
1715 Stagecoach Rd.
Hanson, Kentucky 42413
(502) 825-1533

McClanahan
Publishing House

Contents

Acknowledgments

First and foremost, I would like to thank my wife, Carolyn, for her invaluable help in the preparation of this book. Her expert knowledge in the proper mechanics of the English language made this work much more readable than it would have been otherwise. Also, her companionship and help during many hours of reading and deciphering hundreds of letters in various libraries made the time spent much more enjoyable and the tasks more manageable.

Secondly, I would like to thank my mother, Mildred Burton Ridenour. Because the area around Falls of Rough was her childhood home, she inspired my continuing interest in this location over the years by telling stories about the Green Family. Thanks also to my aunt, Frances Burton Prugh of Silver Spring, Maryland, for allowing me to stay in her home as I completed research at the National Archives, Washington, D. C.

All historians are indebted to the many librarians who took the time and effort in cataloguing the thousands of documents found in large manuscript collections. One of the librarians, now retired, to whom I want to give a special thanks is Penny Harrison. She did a masterful job of cataloguing the nearly eight thousand items in the Jennie Green Collection at the Kentucky Library, Bowling Green, Kentucky. Her organization made access to specific documents in this collection extremely easy. Other librarians that I would especially like to thank are Pat Hodges, Manuscript Librarian, Kentucky

Library, Bowling Green, Kentucky, and Ron Bryant, Kentucky Historical Society Librarian, Frankfort, Kentucky, who repeatedly showed great patience along with an eager attitude when asked to help find some obscure document or fact. And a special thanks goes to Tom Owen, University of Louisville Archivist, for having the forethought almost two decades ago to interview several people acquainted with the Green family. My local librarian, Lisa Wigley, Hopkins County-Madisonville Public Library, Madisonville, Kentucky, was particularly helpful, too, in her willingness to access the Interlibrary Loan System and to go beyond her duty in my search for historic books and documents.

I owe special thanks to Mary O'Neill, present owner of the Green property at Falls of Rough, for taking me into her confidence and allowing me free access to family papers and memorabilia that remain on the site. A historian knows no greater pleasure than to peruse previously "undiscovered" historic documents. She also welcomed me into her home and provided "bed and board" so that my perusals could proceed with convenience.

Most often the student will thank his teacher for some particular help or inspiration, but I would like to thank a former pupil, Duane Bolin, professor of history at Murray State University, Murray, Kentucky. Dr. Bolin's accomplishments, part of which he credits most undeservedly to me, and his words of encouragement have provided the motivation to extend my own accomplishments so that I would be worthy of his respect.

I acknowledge with gratitude the help provided by professors of history Dr. Carol Crowe-Carraco, Dr. Jack Thacker, and Ms. Nancy Baird, librarian, Kentucky Library, Western Kentucky University, Bowling Green, Kentucky. All willingly offered valuable time, expert knowledge, and guidance.

I extend especial appreciation to Leon Sullivan, my patient and diligent computer consultant/collaborator, and also to David Jessup for his technical advice and assistance.

Their help was invaluable.

Without the assistance of these many contributors, my project would not have been possible. I am indebted to them for their interest in history, their generosity, and their words of encouragement. To all of them I am deeply grateful.

Lastly, I would like to fulfill a promise made to my late uncle, Clarence Burton, just a few months before he died in 1994. I promised that if I ever finished this work I would mention his name. He lived all his life within approximately eighteen miles of Falls of Rough and visited the site on many occasions. He enjoyed my interest in the people and places of his era and thus, without realizing it, provided his own encouragement.

Preface

. . . am particularly attracted by the name of your post office—"Falls of Rough." I should think only good things could come from a community that has such a perfectly unusual and delightful name.

(Spencer Shank to Jennie Scott Green, 9 July 1941)

As a very young boy I heard stories of a place in Grayson County, Kentucky,—in my mind, a mysterious place—where a family had lived for more than one hundred years and had become so wealthy that they owned a mansion, thousands of acres of land, several businesses, and a whole town. Yet with all of this information, no one knew much about the family; at least that was the story told to me by my mother, Mildred Burton Ridenour. Reared just a few miles away, she had made several trips as a child to the small community of Falls of Rough.

As the years passed, I graduated from university, began to teach history, and continued to wonder about this place and the "mystery" of the people who had owned and controlled such wealth. Through the years stories about that family continued to pique my interest, particularly when Miss Jennie Green, the last of the direct descendants and owner of the estate, died in 1965. To whom had she willed the property? What would happen to it now? I never really knew the answers, only that someone occupied the premises. And so my unfulfilled wish for answers remained for two and one-half decades.

In 1990 I decided to show my wife the place I had heard so much about and thought of so many times over the years. When I drove up to the front of the old general store, some amount of restoration was evident. Inside I met Mary O'Neill, a third cousin to the late Jennie Green and the inheritress of the property; her friendly smile and easy conversation enabled me to learn that her family would very much like to see the property preserved. Nearing retirement from my teaching career, I saw this situation as a perfect opportunity; I would offer help (whatever that might be) in the restoration effort. A teacher by profession, I also have a background in carpentry, a skill that could come in handy on a 160-year-old site. Soon I began to travel from my home some seventy miles away to help with small fix-up chores: a roof patched here, a window installed there, a bit of paint on this and that.

At the same time Mrs. O'Neill offered me access to family papers going back almost two hundred years, papers that indicated this family, indeed, was not an ordinary one. Either deliberately or coincidentally the family had managed to preserve a large amount of both personal and business correspondence as well as business records. Why not use this material for a master's thesis and, if there proved to be enough, a book? Little did I know then that this project would soon begin to consume most of my thoughts, time, and energy.

Not only was enough information available to fulfill both my literary goals, but also an interesting fact emerged as I continued my research. Some confusion existed as to the identity of Willis Green, the founder of the site that had long intrigued me. As I began to visit libraries to request material about Willis Green, the standard reply, accompanied by expressions of slight perplexity, was that such information surely existed. But then upon examining the usually minute amount presented, I realized some incongruities existed, especially concerning certain dates and political offices held by Willis Green. As my research progressed to other libraries, this confusion of offices and dates prevailed. Did the materials in these libraries contain the story of a single man or of two different men? By now I was hooked. Would I be able to clear up this apparent inconsistency?

Six years, hundreds of hours, and thousands of miles later, I sit in my study with documents, some aged and fragile, strewn around me as I try to put together, from the product of my obsessive search, a Green family biography. It has become apparent that there were, indeed, two different and prominent Kentucky men named Willis Green, one a statesman active in Kentucky's pursuit for statehood and the other a statesman and entrepreneur of Falls of Rough. History has misidentified them either as one man or as father and son. My research indicates that as well as not being the same man, they were also not father and son—and apparently not even related or, at most, only very distantly so. I hope the result of my labor will allow history's proper recognition for Willis Green of Falls of Rough.

After having thoroughly researched the three generations of the Green family of Falls of Rough, I find them worthy of a historical study not only because they were personally involved in much of the Commonwealth's history but also because of the several unusual facts that have emerged. The most curious circumstance is that none of the four children of the last generation ever married, which has led to endless speculation. I have expended great effort trying to unravel this rather unusual family occurrence with, as yet, very few answers. The prevalent rumor that their father's will would disinherit them if they married is unfounded, as the will contains no such reference. However, after investigating the many facets of these four siblings' lives, I have reached my own tentative, personal conclusions; I will leave the reader freedom to do the same. Quite possibly this social anomaly will remain unexplained and forever continue as a source of interesting speculation.

I have written this history in a manner that might be classified by some historians as "old fashioned." There is no composed dialogue, little speculation into the thoughts and motives of participants other than those few identified, and no distortion of chronology other than that necessary for literary expediency. The temptation was considerable to use secondary sources to give answers not found in primary sources but, to ensure the integrity and accuracy of the work, the use of such material was minimal. Although the family retained a vast amount of correspondence and records, most in the period between 1865 and 1900, some time periods and subjects relinquish few or no records; the result is an occasional appearance of inconsistency.[1]

Upon the near-completion of my research, one of my main concerns was that my history would be dull reading because I failed to "dig up" any "juicy" stories. When I expressed this apprehension to Dr. Thomas Clark, noted Kentucky historian and author, who so graciously offered his insight and wisdom, he hastened to remind me that not all history is "juicy." Nevertheless, I hope the reader will find this biography of a remarkable Kentucky family interesting and, perhaps, even engaging.

Chapter One

"Without Any Heritage, but Poverty and an Honest Name"

On Friday 19 July 1844, in Alexandria, District of Columbia, a mass meeting of the Clay Club Whigs brought such great numbers of people that they filled to overflowing the city's public square, many having traveled from the surrounding counties in Virginia and Maryland. The crowd, particularly enlivened on this evening by the smiles and greetings of the many "ladies" present, waited in excited anticipation for the beginning of the night's speeches. The mere mention of the name Henry Clay brought forth great cheers and applause. Then at the appointed hour Lewis McKenzie, President of the Clay Club, began his introduction of the first of the evening's speakers, Representative Willis Green of Kentucky.[1]

At this moment Willis Green was enjoying the height of his political career, one that had begun in his Grayson County, Kentucky, home district some seventeen years earlier. But his political journey might not have progressed to this point if not for his personal and business accomplishments,

Willis Green
Courtesy Mary O'Neill, Falls of Rough

which had earned him credibility and respect. Only a strong sense of adventure and extra measures of ingenuity and ambition, along with frequent risk-taking, had allowed Willis Green such success, for his youth had provided him an inauspicious beginning.

Willis Green — a friend, sometimes "messmate," and political ally of Henry Clay — was born in Madison County, Kentucky, in 1795 to Stephen and Elizabeth Stuart Green. He was only age three when his father died, leaving him and a younger brother and sister, Morgan and Nancy, to the guardianship of his grandfather, also named Stephen. Approximately three years later, between July 1801 and April 1802, their grandfather died, prompting Willis Green to afterward state that he had been orphaned at age seven "without any heritage, but poverty and an honest name." Green spent at least part of his childhood after his grandfather's death in the home of his uncle, Martin Green.[2]

Green's use of the term *poverty* must have been a relative one because he was not left destitute. The full value of his inheritance is difficult to ascertain, but his father's estate, inventoried and appraised in 1798, included several cows, horses, and pigs valued at approximately eigthy-one pounds, plus the value of several slaves. Fourteen years later in 1812, when his father's estate was finally settled, Green inherited his one-third share, which amounted to one mulatto slave, Ben, valued at eighty pounds, plus approximately fifty-three pounds in cash. He also received one sixth of his grandfather's estate in 1813 after the death of his grandmother Jemima. The auction of this estate garnered $580.73, including $30.37 1/2 from Squire Boone for "1 Bed, Beadstead & furniture." [3]

When the United States declared war on Great Britain in 1812, seventeen-year-old Green volunteered. His military experience probably added to his maturity and perhaps also increased his patriotism. But because no diary or letters from him are available, how the conflict affected him is mere speculation, as is his specific role in the war. The only way to know some details of his participation is to chronicle the movements and activities of the military units of which he was a part.

Green joined the two thousand other Kentucky volunteers who mustered into the army at Louisville or at several other locations along the Ohio River. So many Kentuckians volunteered for service that several companies were turned away, causing one of the spurned volunteers to exclaim, "Well, well, Kentucky has often glutted the market with hemp, flour, and tobacco, and now she has done it with volunteers." Four regiments formed immediately, and a fifth organized a short time later under the command of Colonel Samuel South. Green enlisted in this fifth regiment on 18 September 1812 and became a private in Captain Robert A. Sturgus' Company of Kentucky Mounted Volunteer Militia. In early October the volunteers marched to Fort Harrison on the Wabash River in the Indiana Territory. Major General Samuel Hopkins, commander of the troops, had been ordered to exact retribution upon several Kickapoo Indian villages along the Illinois River, whose inhabitants were believed responsible for the massacre of the American forces at Fort Dearborn(Chicago) in mid-July 1812.[4]

Many of the volunteers, including Green, were typically young, undisciplined, and lacking in military training. The recruits drew ten days' provisions and began a march of what they believed would be eighty-five miles; but after traveling for five days and changing directions several times, they began to run low on supplies. Believing the Indian villages still to be several days away, the troops mutinied, and General Hopkins retreated to the fort at Vincennes. Later, however, the fact emerged that at the time of the mutiny the villages actually did remain some sixty to seventy miles away, and the volunteers acquired some vindication. Although it is not known if Green was among the mutineers, he was active during the period from 18 September to 30 October 1812 and received a total of $26.52, which included an allowance of $17.20 for his horse and equipment: a bridle, saddle, powder horn and pouch, tomahawk, and scalp knife.[5]

In July of the next year, with General William Henry Harrison appealing for help, newly elected Governor Isaac Shelby called for volunteers to meet him at Newport on 31 August. He offered a rousing appeal: "I will meet you there in person . . . Fellow citizens! Now is the time to act! and by one decisive blow, put an end to the contest in that quarter." The venerable governor believed three to four thousand Kentuckians would rally to the cause, and he was not disappointed when again great numbers of Kentuckians, including Willis Green, volunteered. Green and fellow volunteers mustered in at Newport, Kentucky, on 31 August 1813, joining the Eleventh Regimental command of Colonel William Williams and the company of Captain Richard C. Holder.[6]

Thirty-five hundred Kentucky volunteers, including the sixty-two-year-old Governor Shelby and eighteen-year-old Willis Green, marched in mid-September 1813 to the region of the upper Ohio, where they joined General Harrison's forces. After taking Detroit on 30 September, Harrison and Shelby pursued British General Henry Proctor, now joined by Shawnee Chief Tecumseh and his forces, up the Thames River. On the morning of 5 October Harrison's and Shelby's forces engaged General Proctor and Tecumseh along the river near Moraviantown. During the ensuing battle, one in which the great Indian leader Tecumseh died, Green suffered a wound to his knee. His exact role in the conflict is unclear as well as the specific cause of his injury, which continued to trouble him throughout his life. In fact, Green often mentioned the affliction later in his political career when he felt doing so would be to his advantage; but the wound did not prevent his continuing service, and on 21 October 1813 he was promoted to Quartermaster Sergeant of the Eleventh Regiment. He mus-

Ann Allen Green
Courtesy Mary O'Neill, Falls of Rough

tered out of the army on 7 November 1813 and received pay of $55.80 for seventy-five days' service, which again included the use of his horse and equipment.[7]

With no particular interest or business connection, Green headed to the excitement of New Orleans, a city rapidly growing as the major shipping outlet for goods produced in Kentucky and other states in the nation's ever-expanding West. While in that city, other than doing the things young men typically do, such as taking a great interest in the eligible young women, he learned the potential profits of the shipping business, particularly in the shipping of tobacco, hemp, lumber, and pork. Although his education is undocumented, he began to practice law there, serving on several occasions as a substitute for attorney Isaac Preston in the collection of overdue notes.[8]

Soon after Green's return to Kentucky in 1818, friends in New Orleans sent him advice about which commodities were selling best. One advised him that tobacco and pork would sell well and that lard from "corn-fed hogs (not mush raised hogs)" would also be profitable. They also recommended against sending corn or whiskey since dealers in these products had been losing money. In a letter dated 1819 another friend reported that flour was bringing ten dollars a barrel, that sugar and cotton prices were good, and that the price of tobacco was down as a result of competition from Europe. Green, now living in Shelbyville, Kentucky, began to ship locally purchased loads of lumber, tobacco, and "his country produce" down the Kentucky River via the Ohio and Mississippi Rivers to New Orleans.[9]

On 24 December 1818 Willis Green married Ann Allen of Shelby County, and in the early 1820s they moved to Hardinsburg. Soon after receiving permission to argue before the Breckinridge County Court in 1822, he resumed his law career. Green also began to purchase land, often in partner-

Ledger, store 1832-1838

ship with Jefferson Jennings, a deputy clerk of Breckinridge County. Green's partnership with Jennings afforded him preemptive knowledge of impending bankruptcy and estate auctions, which enabled the partners to buy land at what could only be called buyers' prices. For example, on 30 June 1826 Green and Jennings bought a 550-acre tract for a total of fifty-five dollars, on 1 July 1826 three hundred acres on Panther Creek for five dollars, and on 5 July 1826 five hundred acres for $55.25. Then on 30 October 1827 Green personally purchased at public auction one half of a 9,830-acre tract of land for sixty-six dollars.[10]

A part of this entrepreneurial land-buying effort was Green's purchase of the land along Rough Creek that would become the site of the present community known as Falls of Rough. On 9 June 1829 Green purchased from William Sebastian, for one thousand dollars, two hundred acres at the falls of Rough Creek known as the "Sebastian mill site." On the site stood a sawmill, gristmill, and distillery.[11]

When Green bought the mill site in 1829, a dispute existed concerning the ownership of the property. Apparently William Sebastian had filed no formal deed transfer when he received the property from his father, Benjamin. (Benjamin Sebastian, a former member of the Kentucky Court of Appeals, had fled to western Kentucky after being implicated in the 1790s plot to deliver Kentucky to the Spanish government.) To further complicate the matter, the elder Sebastian supposedly sold the identical property to one Nathan Anderson for the sum of one thousand dollars at the same time that his son sold it to Green for that amount.

As a result of the lack of a clear title to the property, Green sued Nathan Anderson in Grayson County Chancery Court in Leitchfield. In an affidavit, witness Anselm Watkins answered the question "Did Green induce William Sebastian to sell the property before Benjamin Sebastian did or he would get nothing out of the land?" with "Not that I know of." An additional allegation followed that William Sebastian had an alcohol problem, in fact was a "drunk," and that Green bought the property while Sebastian was intoxicated. Green, representing himself, asked Watkins whether William Sebastian was sober at the time of the purchase; Watkins replied that he was. As a result of this and probably other testimony, Willis Green prevailed, obtaining clear title to the property on and along Rough Creek, later designated Rough River.[12]

This two-hundred-acre tract became the cornerstone of a land and business empire involving a small town and several counties, not to mention other states. By 1831 Green had become one of the largest landowners in the area with approximately 10,800 acres in Grayson and Breckinridge counties.[13]

Tax records suggest that Green finally received the deed to the mill-site property in 1831; soon afterward he upgraded the sawmill and gristmill, opened a blacksmith shop, and increased the inventory of the general store. Then in 1832 he contracted with Robert Armstrong to operate a water-powered wool-carding machine. Green agreed to pay the operator one dollar per day plus board and washing and to provide the assistance of a small boy or girl. Ledgers from the store indicate that the carding machine proved a good business investment, with nearly every account customer taking advantage of it either by bringing wool to be carded or by buying pre-carded rolls of wool. Also quite popular with the customers were the flyings (droppings from the carding process), sometimes used for quilt batting.[14]

The addition of the carding machine, along with a well-stocked general store and the other enterprises, resulted in a very successful and profitable operation. The 1832 ledger for the store lists nearly four hundred credit customers; interestingly, both Benjamin and William Sebastian, former owners of the site, number among these customers. Benjamin's account implies that on several occasions he either brought in items to trade or exchanged work for the goods purchased.[15]

Willis Green's hopes of even greater expansion of the Falls businesses seem apparent in an act dated 7 February 1838 to incorporate the Jefferson Pond Draining Company and Rough Creek Manufacturing Company. To promote the manufacture of "Iron and woolen, cotton and hempen goods and sawing timber," the act reads, "a company for the manufacture thereof at the great falls of Rough Creek is hereby created and established to have corporate existence for 20 years by the name of Rough Creek Manufacturing Co. with capital of $100,000." Green received permission to sell stock in this company, whose incorporation became legal with the signatures of the leaders of the Kentucky House and Senate as well as the governor and secretary of state. How much this "conglomerate" affected profits at the Falls is uncertain, but according to an affidavit in an 1848 or 1849 lawsuit, Green stated that the businesses, in the six or seven years prior to the suit, had made a profit of forty thousand dollars.[16]

In the late 1830s Green probably invested some of these profits, along with the proceeds from the sale of several thousand acres of land, into building a new house (or the complete remodeling of an already existing structure) as well as to improving some of his mills. The house underwent remodeling again in the late 1870s, leaving little evidence of its former appearance; however, an 1839 contractor's list of finish materials offers some idea of its structure. The house consisted of two stories (perhaps a story and a half) with several rooms and at least two chimneys and three fireplaces. The use of rose blocks (decorative carvings at the top corners of door and window frames) and pilasters indicates that the house was well appointed.[17]

Green, ever the progressive entrepreneur, soon sought to add to the success of his businesses. In the mid-1840s he considered installing water turbines in the mills to increase work capacity and thereby add to their profitability. One intact water turbine remains today—under the gristmill—and iron fragments testify that two other such wheels provided power for the saw and carding mills. However, though no record certifies that Green installed the turbines at this time, evidence clearly exists that by the mid-1840s he had rebuilt his mills and made other improvements; in January 1844 Congressman Green, in Washington, received word from the man overseeing his sawmill that his mill had "new saws" and was doing fine. Because many mills converted from the much slower sash saw (a single blade which is held in a frame and reciprocates vertically through the log) to the more efficient circular saw during this time, whether *new* meant *modern* or *just- purchased* is uncertain; either, however, was an improvement.[18]

With the improved efficiency and expansion of his businesses came the need for labor, supplied in some cases by local day laborers or indenturers, but most often by slaves. In 1824 Green owned at least one slave (perhaps more), and over the next few years he purchased additional chattel, eventually owning a dozen or more.[19]

In addition to being a businessman, Willis Green continued his law practice and by 1827 had also become involved in politics. His numerous commitments kept him away from home for long periods and occupied an increasing amount of his time. And with his mercantile establishments at Hudsonville and Caneyville as well as at the Falls, he recognized a need to lessen his business demands. Consequently, he entered into a business partnership in 1835 with long-time land-speculating partner Jefferson Jennings. This partnership involved Jennings' management of most, if not all, of Green's businesses. Green trusted his new partner, for when he had first met Jennings, although Green believed him to be "a man of limited means," he also "had the reputation of being a good clerk and honest man with a smooth face."

Several years later, however, Green was in Breckinridge County Chancery Court defending himself against the partner whose reputation and appearance had proved misleading. Jennings accused Green of refusing to reimburse him for expenses incurred in the business operations during a period between 1837 and 1845 when Green was seldom at home. Green denied the debt and testified that his partner had taken advantage of his protracted absences and the intimate knowledge he held of Green's finances. They dissolved the partnership in 1848 or 1849, but the dispute was not resolved until 1864, after both men died; descendants of each man shared jointly in whatever property and real estate remained.[20]

From his rather humble beginnings as a Madison County orphan, Green developed into not only a successful man but a wealthy one as well. The sense of adventure that took him into battle during the War of 1812 had perhaps also drawn the young man to New Orleans, where he practiced law and, most importantly, began to cultivate his entrepreneurial genius. With that seed of enterprise, he returned to Kentucky along Rough Creek on the boundary of Grayson and Breckinridge Counties to build his "empire." While doing so, he once again drew upon his patriotic spirit to serve in both state and national governments. The attributes that helped make Willis Green a wealthy landowner and successful businessman at Falls of Rough also played a distinct role in his eighteen-year political career.

Chapter Two

"Old Wheelhorse"

Willis Green's agrarian and entrepreneurial background formed much of his political philosophy; however, the state's prevailing political climate greatly shaped the development of that philosophy. In 1827, when Green entered politics, Kentucky was emerging from the most tumultuous decade in the state's history, with the possible later exception of the cataclysmic years of the Civil War. The issues that divided the state during this period included the fight between the relief (New Court) and anti-relief (Old Court) parties and the realignment of the national political parties.

To a great extent the division between the relief and anti-relief parties resulted from the national monetary panic of 1819, itself a consequence of the chartering of the Second Bank of the United States in 1816. The bank, after a short period of speculation, required that notes held on state banks be redeemed with specie, which forced many debtors into bankruptcy or near-bankruptcy. This hardship provoked the debtor citizens of the Commonwealth to clamor for the legislature to take some action that would relieve them of their burden.

In response to the call for financial relief, the legislature in 1817-1818 chartered forty independent banks and later added six more. Each of these new banks issued paper money, resulting in the state's being flooded with this currency. Speculation began anew with even greater vigor than before, but as the bubble of speculation quickly burst, many Kentuckians found themselves more deeply in debt than in the previous years. To these debtors there seemed no alternative but to broaden the replevin laws, allowing debtors to postpone payment until a later date. The result of the attempt to expand such laws was a fight between those who wanted relief in this form and those who thought such acts not only irresponsible but also unconstitutional. Supporters of relief as the proper and necessary policy began to migrate to the Democrat Republican Party (later known as Jackson Democrats), while anti-relief advocates moved toward the National Republican Party (later known as the Clay or Whig Party).[1]

Willis Green entered Kentucky politics amidst this political and social turmoil. A budding young entrepreneur with several businesses, he quite naturally became a follower of Henry Clay and the National Republicans, whose principles benefited those endeavors. This party and Clay's "American System" supported higher protective tariffs and internal improvements, definite advantages for merchants and shippers of products like tobacco and hemp. Protective tariffs reduced competition and resulted in greater profitability; internal improvements, such as constructing canals and dams, clearing obstructions from rivers and, later, building railroads and roads, facilitated these products' shipment to their markets.

Green was elected to the Kentucky Senate in 1827 from the Sixteenth Senatorial District, containing the counties of Ohio, Daviess, and Breckinridge. The Senate convened on 3 December 1827, but Green did not take his seat until 19 December, perhaps because the unusually rainy weather and resulting high water made travel difficult. On 21 December Green, his motives unclear, made a motion to "bring in a bill" for the benefit of Alfred and Isaac Shelby and immediately accepted assignment to a committee to accomplish that task. On 27 December he accepted a second committee appointment to examine the Auditor's Office for the year 1825 on behalf of the Senate. Even though Green was a member of these committees, he failed to vote from 19 December 1827 through 1 January 1828; no explanation is evident. On 21 January, however, he reported from a committee "a bill from the House of Representatives, entitled, 'an act to amend an act incorporating the Hartford Manufacturing Company.'" The bill passed with an amendment by a vote of 26 to 4, and Green reported back to the House for its concurrence with the amendment. The Senate session ended 13 February 1828.

Green was again a member of the Senate, now also representing Hancock County, in 1829 and 1830, but when his term expired in 1831, he briefly left the political scene. Five years later, in 1836, when he again ran for office, his Grayson County constituency elected him to the Kentucky House of Representatives, where he served one term.[2]

After serving in both houses of the state legislature, Green sought a seat in the U. S. House of Representatives. However, the late 1830s was not the most propitious time to seek political office in Kentucky, especially as an "anti-relief" Whig, for Kentucky was again recovering from a period of financial instability, much of which resulted from President Andrew Jackson's policies. After Jackson vetoed the rechartering of the Bank of the United States in 1832 and then subsequently flooded the state's financial institutions (his so-called "pet banks") with the federal government's money, speculation once more ran wild. Then his issuance of the "specie circular" in 1836 tightened credit, causing financial ruin for many Kentuckians. But this time the state legislature refused to acquiesce to the "relief" clamor, although many citizens suffered as a result.[3]

Green's first attempt at national office was in 1839 for the Sixth Congressional seat vacated by John Calhoon, who had moved to Missouri. A decided underdog to opponent John L. Hardin of Hardin County, Green used liberally the "typical" campaign tactics. He employed one of the most common ones: on election day he made available a generous supply of good whiskey to mellow out any lingering opposition that might otherwise hinder the "proper" vote. This tact proved successful, as the sheriffs of the Sixth Congressional District counties certified Green the winner on 19 August 1839.[4]

Green took his seat when the Twenty-sixth Congress convened in December of 1839 and immediately became involved in a controversy concerning several disputed seats. Over the next few weeks he participated in the routine business of the House, but not until President Martin Van Buren's administration reintroduced the Subtreasury Bill into Congress did he stir to action. This bill, first introduced in the Twenty-fifth Congress where it passed the Senate but failed in the House, would have put government money in independent vaults under the control of government officials. The administration tried anew to gain passage of this highly controversial bill, and once more the Senate experienced heated debate, with Kentucky's Henry Clay putting forth a gallant effort to kill the bill. Despite Clay's political savvy and stirring orations, the bill passed the Senate on 23 January 1840.[5]

Over the next five months the House debated this bill, with Green one of its more adamant opponents. Reminiscent of his hero, Green on 30 June 1840 spoke for nearly an hour, enumerating a dozen or so reasons for his opposition. The most compelling arguments included his beliefs that, first, passage of such a bill would increase the patronage of the President, thereby allowing him to punish his opponents; secondly, workers would be paid in paper money but have to pay the government in specie, resulting in an undue burden on laborers. His further belief that the result of the bill would "pamper and enrich the office holder" prompted Green to compare this legislation to Louis XIV's declaration that "the king is the State."[6]

The most stinging criticism in Green's speech came from his labeling the Subtreasury Bill a piece of "political quack machinery." The ultimate solution he offered to such an "odious scheme" would be the triumph in the upcoming fall presidential election of General William Henry Harrison, the great general of the Northwest campaign and the Battle of the Thames, over incumbent Martin Van Buren. And with the mention of the latter conflict, Green invoked whatever benefits might then or later result from his association with Harrison and his own engagement at age eighteen in that battle. Green must have believed the reference to the Battle of the Thames and his resulting wound an effective tactic, for he ordered four thousand copies of the speech printed, presumably for use in his next campaign. Nonetheless, despite the valiant fight against it by Green and his Whig colleagues in the House, the Subtreasury Bill passed by a vote of 124 to 107, and President Van Buren signed it into law on 4 July 1840.[7]

A few months later Green found himself in another contentious situation. On 10 December 1840, at the beginning of the Twenty-sixth Congress' second session, he accepted appointment to the Committee on Public Expenditure, an assignment that might have resulted from his articulate opposition to the Subtreasury Bill. His position on this committee kept him involved throughout the session in the many controversial economic issues before Congress, including the government issuance of treasury notes, the Bankruptcy Act, and the tariff.[8]

During the Twenty-sixth Congressional session Green lived at Mrs. E. S. Arguelle's boarding house, where Henry Clay also resided. The two men became friends, developing a political and personal relationship that strengthened over the next several years. At that point Green began to align himself even more closely with Clay's personal Whig philosophy and, along with fellow Whigs, became excited about their prospects in the upcoming Twenty-seventh Congress, when they looked forward to not only having the presidency but also control of both houses of Congress.

In the meantime, before Inauguration Day, Green introduced several petitions and resolutions. One of these, introduced on 14 January 1841 and based on the Whig campaign promise to make the government more financially responsible, asked the Committee on Ways and Means to inquire into levying duties on imports such as wine, silk, linen, and other luxury items. The measure, seeking to pay debts incurred by Van Buren's treasury notes, failed by a vote of eighty to eighty-six, but Green reintroduced an amended version of the resolution on 5 February then withdrew it after being called on a point of order. Believing the Whigs should fulfill their campaign pledges, he reintroduced the resolution before the Twenty-seventh Congress, but with no evidence of success.[9]

With the duty of fiscal responsibility an ever-present concern, Green delivered a speech in the House on 18 February 1841 which presented strong arguments against the government's three branch mints. He argued that these facilities were a waste of taxpayers' money because the Philadelphia mint could print and coin all the money necessary with the equipment and workers it presently retained. Such economy would eliminate the $380,000 annual expense required to keep the branch mints in operation.

Furthermore, Green argued that these branches, each under the control of an independent superintendent, prevented a uniformly valued currency, a standard he and fellow Whigs believed necessary. He queried, "How can we excuse ourselves to our constituents, to our country, to our consciences, for throwing away the public money on a litter of pet mints?" Green further alleged that the only reason for these mints' existence was political patronage. Although some of his colleagues admonished him to postpone the pursuit in this matter until Harrison was inaugurated and the Whigs gained strength in Congress, Green insisted the time to act was at hand and proclaimed his intention to keep Whig campaign promises to the "letter and spirit."[10]

Thursday, 4 March 1841 was by all accounts a glorious day for the Whigs. At the head of Harrison's inaugural procession marched a small contingent of veterans of the War of 1812, with General Leslie Combs of Kentucky dressed "in the costume of a Kentucky volunteer, and such a one as General Harrison wore while commanding on the northwestern frontier." These veterans proceeded to the White House for refreshments and then to Gadsby's Hotel, where they listened to a speech by General Combs. Green, proud of his war service, was surely among this revered contingent of veterans. Unfortunately for the Whigs, however, the euphoria of victory did not endure; on 4 April, just one month after taking office, President Harrison died of pneumonia. Some attributed his fatal illness to a combination of fatigue caused by the onslaught of office seekers and the failure to wear adequate clothing on the cold, rainy inaugural day.[11]

During the month between Harrison's inauguration and his death, several Whigs, and particularly Clay, disagreed with increasing fervor about cabinet appointments. Clay thought Harrison should appoint some of the Kentuckian's personal supporters to key positions, and when Harrison failed to comply with those wishes (partially because of Daniel Webster's intervention), Clay became bellicose and dictatorial, sometimes over seemingly insignificant issues. One of these episodes occurred on 9 March when a verbal battle erupted between Clay and Senator William R. King of Alabama involving the dismissal of Senate Printer Francis Blair. As it continued, the debate became a question not about the dismissal of Blair, but instead about both King's and Clay's characters; it concluded with what appeared to be King's challenging Clay to a duel. The Senate sergeant-at-arms intervened, arresting both King and Clay as well as Willis Green, whose reason for being in the chamber and involved in the dispute is unclear. The next day both Clay and Green appeared in Washington County, D. C., court, where they each posted a five-thousand-dollar bond and agreed to "keep the peace of the United States toward all persons, and particularly towards WILLIAM R. KING."[12]

In the summer of 1841 Green campaigned to retain his congressional seat, which represented the counties of Hardin, Green, Hart, Meade, Breckinridge, and Grayson, for the term that would expire at the end of this Twenty-sixth session of Congress. Because several prospective candidates made an effort to gain the Whig nomination from Green's district, a convention met on County Court Day, 29 March 1841, in Elizabethtown to select one candidate. Several candidates dropped out, and Green won the convention's approval as the party's standard bearer. Because district political opposition developed and duties prevented his presence there, Green immediately sent constituents a circular outlining his positions on issues facing the Twenty-sixth Congress. Most of these positions followed the Whig party line or, more precisely, the philosophy of Clay.

One of the six or seven issues included in his circular concerned the government's issuance of treasury notes, which both Clay and Green opposed. Green, a fiscal conservative, believed that such notes would lead to overspending and result in increased government debt. He also held the opinion that issuance of the notes was not the most cost-effective way for the government to borrow money. In fact, he described the strategy as nothing more than a "shinplaster" and recommended "a direct old fashioned loan."

The circular also included Green's advocacy of a United States Bank powerful enough to regulate currency as it had once done due to its "presence of responsibility." Such regulation, he predicted, would produce a stable and uniform currency of especial benefit to his Kentucky constituents, allowing the producer to sell goods and pay off debts at widely distant locations without a loss of profit. As the situation existed, each bank issued its own notes, which resulted in a disparate currency value between banks. According to Green, a Kentucky producer might sell his goods in New Orleans for a paper currency five percent lower than the value of his own, then pay his debts in Philadelphia or New York, where the currency might be three or four percent higher, resulting in a total loss of as much as eight or nine percent. He also did not support the idea of subjecting the economy to only a gold and silver currency, as enough specie could not be in circulation, he believed, to support all necessary business transactions.

Another issue Green addressed in the circular and one on which he and Clay stood together was the imposition of a tariff to raise revenues, and Green was adamant that a number of luxury items be included. Congress had defeated his earlier attempts to introduce a similar resolution, but he continued to argue its need. He maintained that the Compromise Tariff of 1833, which gave concessions to the interest of northern manufacturers by exempting many luxury items from tariff duties, was appropriate only so long as no treasury deficit existed. But the Van Buren administration's use of treasury notes had incurred debt that changed the treasury's status, creating a need for such a tax. Green held that both "the South" and "Northern manufacturers" should be willing to enact such a tariff because it would be a tax only upon "wealth and prodigality."

Willis Green usually sided with Clay on Whig policy, but he disagreed with his mentor on at least one plank of Clay's "American System,"—the national government's role in financing internal improvements. Clay argued in favor of the national government's responsibility for public works, but while his opponents cited constitutional barriers to the plan (specifically, the power of the states versus that of the federal government), Green based his opposition on economic grounds, offering as one argument the discrepancy in road construction costs. The national government had built the Cumberland Road, for example, at a cost of $14,000 per mile, but a similar mile of state road cost only about $6,000. He further argued that internal improvements financed by the federal government greatly increased the "patronage and power" of the executive branch of the U. S. Government.[13]

Another issue on which Green and Clay disagreed dramatically centered on the Bankruptcy Act, an act allowing an individual to declare insolvency. The bill provoked impassioned discussion between the two men and was a topic of their conversation for years. Two years after the debate in Congress, Clay wrote Green defending his position. The tone of the letter suggests he wanted his friend to fully understand why he (Clay) had supported the Bankruptcy Act so staunchly and had been willing to do so regardless of his friends' stands or the Kentucky legislature's directive on the issue. In the 1843 letter Clay recalled that when "we boarded together . . . You were firmly, constantly, I thought almost obstinately opposed to its passage, and in favor of its repeal." He reminded his former "messmate" that although he had not tried to persuade Green to his point of view, Green had nonetheless tried to "convert" him, with Clay's adding, "but we both retained our respective opinions."[14]

Near the end of the extra session of the Twenty-sixth Congress, both Houses passed the Bankruptcy Bill and President Tyler signed it into law. Such great numbers of people took advantage of this act, particularly in Kentucky, where large speculative debts had occurred over the previous several years, that much of the Commonwealth's populace felt a threat to the "protection of property." Many Kentuckians were so concerned that they instructed their senators to vote for its repeal, a directive Clay ignored. Six months later the House voted in favor of a repeal bill while the Senate refused to do so, with Clay's vote against it the decisive one.[15]

Between House debates, impassioned issues, and committee assignments, Willis Green occupied himself with pursuits of lesser national import. Because they submitted themselves to voter approval every two years, members of the House were obliged to undertake sundry concerns for the people in their districts. Such matters ranged from petitions for veterans' pensions to relief from debt, but most often dealt with patronage jobs. One such request illustrates the reputation Green had earned regarding his diligent ability to deliver such favors; that the correspondent contacted him testifies to the faith Green had engendered. A former constituent hoped to accomplish the appointment of an individual to the District Marshal's Office in northern Mississippi. He wrote that he "thought proper . . . to call on the Old Wheel Horse who I know never fails when he makes an effort."[16]

Green's apparent success in such accommodations and his dedicated effort to effectively represent his constituents, along with a tide of Whig popularity, probably helped to win his reelection in 1841. Whigs constituted all except two of the representatives from Kentucky to the Twenty-seventh Congress, which devoted much of its business to the Tariff and the Distribution Act.[17]

During the second session of the Twenty-seventh Congress, Green was a fellow boarding house resident with John J. Crittenden, former attorney general and now a senator as the result of his election by the Kentucky legislature to Clay's recently resigned seat. During this session Green continued to introduce resolutions to add luxury items to the tariff to help lower the treasury deficit. He introduced one such resolution on 21 March 1842, but records give no evidence that any of his tariff resolutions ever succeeded in becoming bills. Then during the third session Green introduced, among others, a resolution to have the Committee of Ways and Means to "bring in a bill" to finance removal of obstructions in "western waters."[18]

In the spring of 1843, Willis Green began to campaign for his late-summer reelection to Congress. As a result of congressional redistricting, Kentucky contained ten districts instead of the previous thirteen. Green, consequently representing the Second District instead of the Sixth, relinquished the counties of Hardin, Green, and Hart while retaining Breckinridge, Meade, and Grayson, but added Christian, Muhlenberg, Henderson, Daviess, Ohio, Butler, Hancock, and Edmondson. This change increased his district both in population and area while shifting it farther west in the state.[19]

Green faced three opponents in his bid to again obtain his party's nomination: William Sterrett, David Banks, and James F. Buckner. At the district convention held at Hartford on 5 June, he won on the first ballot over his closest rival, William Sterrett, by a nearly two-to-one majority. Such a wide margin of victory prompted the *Frankfort Commonwealth* to proclaim that "the perfect harmony and good feeling prevailed. Mr. G. will leave his Locofoco competitors out of sight." (The Whigs termed most Democrats during this period as Locofocos.) However, this early optimism soon faced a severe test.[20]

During the summer, Whig campaign efforts intensified because the Democratic Party had broken into several factions and many of the Whig candidates not only faced Locofoco opponents but also independent opponents. As in previous elections, the party invited both local and national Whig candidates to barbecues in several Kentucky locations and throughout the country. Additionally, Whig candidates campaigned not only for their offices but also for Henry Clay's election to the Presidency, a certainty in the minds of all Whigs. That the party had not yet officially chosen Clay as its candidate in no way lessened the Whigs' zeal.[21]

The margin of victory or defeat in the 1843 election was extremely narrow in many of Kentucky's districts, with the closest being Green's 234-vote margin over Locofoco candidate Thomas C. McCreery. So much for those early flushes of campaign optimism! Whigs controlled only five of the state's ten districts instead of the eleven of thirteen in the previous Congress. The late summer elections should have been a wake-up call not only to Kentucky's but to all Whigs as well.[22]

After reelection to his third term in Congress, Green campaigned in earnest for Henry Clay. Green not only chaired the Executive Committee of the Whig members of Congress, but he and close friend Representative Garrett Davis of Kentucky also comprised a committee to promote Clay's presidential bid by distributing Whig literature. Green also performed personal errands for Clay, who spent most of the campaign at his home in Lexington, by forwarding mail, verifying his handwriting to prevent forgeries and, on at least one occasion, procuring him rooms for a short stay in Washington. In a 24 August letter Clay acknowledged the extent of Green's sacrifice of time and effort in completing such tasks: "I perceive you continue to have your hands full. Don't you apprehend that Mrs. Green will apply for a divorce."[23]

Green's primary effort on Clay's behalf was the distribution of Whig literature to the various Clay Clubs and election committees where the Whigs thought opposition to be strongest. Following a common campaign tactic of the mid-1800s, he flooded the selected districts with party papers, such as printed speeches, newspaper articles, and personal letters outlining Clay's and fellow Whigs' positions. Some candidates, though, resorted to more creative methods of conveying their political messages. One Whig campaign worker in Kentucky requested that Green send political material quickly in order to combat a Locofoco who was apparently sending garden seeds, "to the amount of several bushels," to farmers through the mail.[24]

But the real highlights of the political season were the personal speeches of candidates and their campaign workers. Crowds came from great distances and stood for interminable hours to listen to oratory by and about their favorite candidate. During such an occasion on the evening of 19 July, amid the buzz of political excitement and the almost fair-like atmosphere, Willis Green received an introduction and began his speech to the Clay Club of Alexandria in the District of Columbia. Acknowledging that the citizens of Alexandria could not vote for President, he insisted they nevertheless could influence the election by their continued support of the Whig Party. In his oration he asked the audience to consider what the Locofocos had ever done for them except to disregard the will of the people and sell them out "to suit the peculiar opinions of the Southern chivalry—of South Carolina and her Nullifiers and disunionists." Then making accusations of unsuccessful monetary policies and failure to support the Tariff of 1842, Green threw several jabs at former President Martin Van Buren, Democratic presidential candidate James K. Polk, and President John Tyler, by then a Whig outcast. He followed by outlining the Whigs' superior philosophy on the issues of the day.

As his speech came to a close, Green moved away from the detailed litany of policy and toward anecdotes of caustic humor and wit aimed at Clay's opponents. One such yarn concerned a woodchuck that returned to his den to find an intruder. When he realized the intruder did not smell, talk, or look like a woodchuck, he threw the "Polk-at" out, clearly a reference to James Polk's efforts to appear "Whiggish." A second anecdote dealt with the attempt of Polk supporters to

associate Polk with Andrew Jackson by giving him the nick-
name "Young Hickory." Green questioned the possibility of
such a correlation: "Young Hickory, eh? . . . I have often heard
of budding and grafting trees of different species, but I never
yet knew that a polk stalk could be grafted on a hickory
stump." Green concluded his speech by congratulating the
"ladies" of the audience for being such staunch supporters,
offering them the Whigs' thanks, and expressing confidence
that in their hands the "Whig cause, and every other cause, is
always safe."[25]

Whigs were certain that Clay would win the election,
so certain that long-time Kentucky Whig notable Ben Hardin
exclaimed, "All hell can't stop his election if he lives and I
think that providence will prolong and protect his valuable
life." "Hell," indeed! When the fall election results came in,
Clay had lost, leaving Whigs disappointed and baffled, even
astounded. Clay won Kentucky by a margin of only ten thousand votes, and even though he did rather well in most northern states, he lost the key state of New York. Green and his
fellow Whigs had been overly optimistic in their predictions.
Perhaps their hearts had overruled their political judgment,
particularly in Kentucky and other southern states where
Clay's stand against the annexation of Texas and his less-than-
enthusiastic support of slavery had cost him votes.[26]

Although they had lost the presidential election and
had not done especially well in many local elections, the
Whigs were nevertheless proud of their stands on issues and,
particularly, of Clay, whom they continued to revere. On 11
March 1845 Green received thanks from Howard House of
the New York City's Central Clay Committee for his efforts on
behalf of Clay and the Whig Party. In addition, the committee asked him to deliver to Clay a commemorative copy of a
speech that Clay had presented in New York City on 4 March
1844. Green personally delivered the speech to his friend,
who acknowledged its receipt in a return letter to the

Committee.[27]

In his consuming effort to effect Clay's election, Green may have neglected to stay sufficiently in touch with local party members and his own constituency. When his House seat came up for reelection in 1845, he failed to obtain his party's nomination, which designated instead a young Hartford lawyer, John H. McHenry. This turn of events, which transpired with Green in Washington and apparently unaware of the political challenge, caused several district party members to fear that more than one Whig candidate would be on the ballot. However, that fear did not materialize because when Green learned that his party had not chosen him, he graciously honored the party's decision. His unselfish dedication to the Whig cause must have been renowned, as the *Louisville Journal* reported, "Such a course is entirely characteristic of him. He always prefers the good of the Whig cause to the advancement of his own individual interests, and thus proves the sincerity of his patriotism." Green's selflessness achieved its purpose, and McHenry won the election.[28]

In 1849 Green intimated that he would again accept the party's nomination for Congress; however, he stipulated he wanted the nomination without having to "submit to convention." The party did not fulfill his wish and he never again held public office. But Green remained an esteemed and prominent political figure in his district, as evidenced by a request that he make a few remarks at an Independence Day celebration in 1859. In doing so he compared the spirit and dedication of the founding fathers and soldiers of the Revolution to that of the ancient Spartans, then concluded by admonishing the audience to replicate their dedication.[29]

With Willis Green's failure to gain nomination in 1845, he was without a political office for the first time in nearly eighteen years—except for a brief time in the 1830s—and could devote himself entirely to his many business enterprises at Falls of Rough. He had left these businesses in the care of others, and they desperately needed his personal attention. He had also "acquired" a family by taking in his deceased brother Morgan's four children: Elizabeth, Malvina, Napoleon, and Lafayette, all of whom had recently lived with their widowed father near Rushville, Illinois. When their father died, in the mid-1840s, the four teens or near-teens came to live at Falls of Rough with Willis and Ann Green, who had no children. Over the next few years the two girls married and moved away; Napoleon worked for a short time for a railroad company but died in 1855 at the age of twenty, apparently a victim of tuberculosis, without ever showing much interest in the businesses at the Falls. However, Lafayette soon showed promise as a businessman and subsequently received grooming as the heir apparent to the growing business empire at Falls of Rough.[30]

In the late 1850s Green, in his early sixties and experiencing debilitating health problems, moved with his wife to Corpus Christi, Texas. His specific health problems are unknown, but a warmer climate held hopeful benefits for his many "aches and pains." Whether he realized his destiny when he moved to Texas, his health never allowed him to return to the Falls. He wrote to Lafayette on 4 June 1860 indicating that he hoped his nephew was "making good speeches" (a reference to Lafayette's budding political career). Willis left no doubt that he considered Lafayette the recipient of his business and political legacy.[31]

Willis Green died on 20 June 1862 in Corpus Christi. Because the Civil War was raging at the time, Lafayette was unable to travel to Texas until 1867 to return his uncle's body to Kentucky. And though his wife wanted her husband returned to Hardinsburg for burial, his body was instead interred in 1868 in Cave Hill Cemetery in Louisville, Kentucky. Ann continued to live at Falls of Rough until her death in March 1877.[32]

Willis Green's life had begun at a time when Kentucky was in its infancy, and he had prospered through Kentucky's early years. He was not just a bystander of the times but an active participant in several key events: the battles of the War of 1812, the political turmoil of the years of conflict in the state over monetary policy, and the great political career of one of Kentucky's and the nation's most distinguished statesmen, Henry Clay. Not only was he involved actively in the political arena of the state but also in the development of Kentucky's economy through his entrepreneurial spirit. But these achievements were only the beginning. Willis Green's nephew and heir, Lafayette, continued his example and built an exemplary legacy of his own.

Lafayette Green, circa 1880
Courtesy Mary O'Neill, Falls of Rough

"Persevering Industry and Ambition"

afayette Green was about ten years old when he went to live with his uncle at Falls of Rough. As he grew to manhood amidst the bustle of a growing empire, he learned quickly the elements that made such an enterprise function and grow, specifically dedication and attention to detail. Also apparent early was his competence to assume the management of his uncle's diverse ventures. An ailing Willis Green wrote from Texas to twenty-four year-old Lafayette, "You are my only hope among my family to represent me & be a credit to my name after I am gone." He added that all Lafayette needed to be a "first rate man" was "persevering industry and ambition to make a man of talents." Lafayette not only fulfilled his uncle's aspirations but, over the next half century, transcended them, leaving his own children an even greater legacy, one that might have been so all consuming it proved nearly impossible to continue.[1]

The specifics of Lafayette's early education are undocumented, but by the age of nineteen or twenty he was already an active participant in the business affairs of his uncle. Some of his earliest duties involved selling products produced at the Falls—lumber, grain, tobacco—in various markets along the Ohio River, such as Evansville and Louisville, and at Rumsey on the Green River. Lafayette also made at least two trips to New Orleans aboard flatboats loaded with lumber sawed at his uncle's mill. His primary responsibility was to escort the lumber safely to its market and then receive payment, whereupon he returned home on foot or, on one trip, on a horse purchased for that purpose. On another occasion he was responsible for hiring out two of Willis' slaves. Lafayette also apparently apprenticed for a short time at a retail establishment, Baxter and Brothers, in Louisville.[2]

While working as an agent for his uncle in Rumsey in 1854, Lafayette studied law, subsequently spending two years, probably 1856-57, in the law office of J. W. Bickers of Rumsey. He eventually earned his credentials for the practice of law and years later spent much of his time in its occupation. Sometime during or shortly after his law apprenticeship, Lafayette became involved in politics.[3]

Following in his uncle's political, though not necessarily his philosophical, footsteps, Lafayette successfully ran in 1859 as a Democrat for a seat in the Kentucky House of Representatives to represent Grayson County. Meeting the House requirement age of twenty-four years by only two months, he was perhaps one of the youngest members ever to sit in that legislative body. He took his seat when the legislature convened on 5 December 1859 and accepted appointment to three standing committees: Sinking Fund, Corporate Institutions, and Court of Appeals.[4]

The year of the 1860 presidential election must have been an interesting one for Lafayette, for he was a delegate to the Democratic Presidential Nominating Convention in Charleston, South Carolina. Lafayette arrived in Charleston around 15 April and lodged at the Mills House in rooms

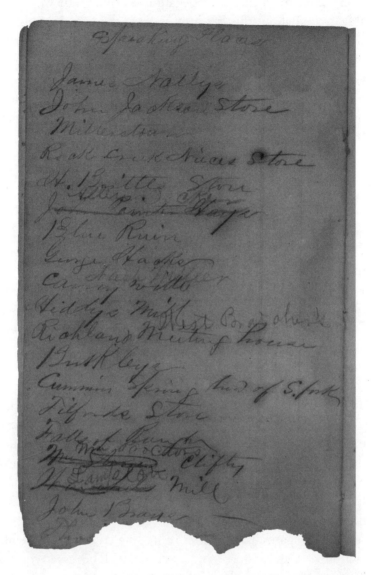

Lafayette Green's speaking locations during his 1859 campaign
Courtesy Kentucky Library, Bowling Green, Kentucky

reserved for the Kentucky delegation. Although he was probably excited about this first venture into the national political arena, the wish of his custodial aunt that he not be a delegate must have tempered Lafayette's enthusiasm somewhat. Ann Green expressed her concern that the political divisions in the party, particularly over slavery, "will incur danger from each side." But Lafayette would not allow his aunt's fears to interfere with his political plans.[5]

The convention convened on 23 April and immediately developed the contentious atmosphere that political forecasters had predicted; after a floor fight over the party's platform, several southern states withdrew. And when, after fifty-seven ballots, the remaining delegation refused to give any candidate a two-thirds majority, the convention adjourned with plans to meet two months later, on 18 June, in Baltimore.[6]

Lafayette was again in attendance when the National Democratic Convention reconvened and began its sessions in Baltimore's Front Street Theatre. After three days of bickering over the credentials of some delegates, particularly those from the states that had seceded from the Charleston Convention, this convention began to collapse. In addition, several states' delegates, including some from Kentucky, objected to the Credentials Committee's decisions concerning delegate seating. On 23 June, Kentucky delegate G. A. Caldwell informed the president of the convention, Caleb Cushing, that ten of Kentucky's delegates were withdrawing. Lafayette and nine fellow delegates issued a statement to the convention: "We deem it inconsistent with our duty to ourselves and our constituents to participate further in its [the convention's] deliberations. Our reasons for so doing will be given to the Democracy of Kentucky." After the protesters' departure, the remaining delegates succeeded in nominating Illinois' Stephen A. Douglas as their presidential candidate.[7]

One week later Lafayette and his nine associates convened at the Maryland Institute with other delegates who had either seceded from the Front Street Convention or had not received admission there. With twenty-one states represented, this convention gave 81 votes on the first ballot to Vice President John C. Breckinridge of Kentucky and 24 votes to Senator Daniel S. Dickinson of New York, who subsequently gave his votes to Breckinridge. The convention nominated General Joseph Lane of Oregon as its vice-presidential candidate and then adjourned "sine die." The party separation between the Douglas and Breckinridge factions, along with an earlier withdrawal of delegates from several southern states, was instrumental in the eventual election of Republican Abraham Lincoln to the Presidency in 1861.[8]

The combination of the Democratic defeat, particularly the defeat of Kentucky's Breckinridge, in the fall presidential election and the looming question of Kentucky's secession from the Union threw the Commonwealth's politics into considerable confusion. An extremist faction of Kentucky's Democratic Party clamored to exercise the right of a state to secede, while the faction consisting of Breckinridge followers and some old-line Whigs tried to find a more amicable solution to the secession problem. When a special session of the General Assembly met on 6 May 1861 to deal with the secession crisis, Lafayette apparently did not take his seat or, at the very least, did not vote on any bills. Whether the confused political situation resulting from the country's civil unrest was in any way responsible for Lafayette's lack of participation remains unclear.[9]

Even though both Lafayette and his uncle were deeply involved in politics and held definite convictions on political issues, including slavery and states' rights, a puzzling lack of correspondence exists among family members in regard to the Civil War. This absence of reference seems to suggest that the War affected the Green family and operations at the Falls much less than it did many others. The few existing references more often pertain to anxieties over what might happen rather than what actually occurred. Ann Green wrote to Lafayette that she worried soldiers would "strip everything" from the Falls. She also indicated that Federal troops surrounding Henderson had prevented Lafayette's sisters from leaving that city and returning to their homes in Rumsey. In the only reference to any fighting in the Falls area, Ann informed Lafayette that locals had reported guerrillas in the area; a small skirmish had resulted in one man's horse shot through the nose and a man wounded, though not mortally. Records fail to indicate whether Lafayette personally played any direct part in the war, either as a soldier, a politician, or a businessman.[10]

Lafayette Green did not seek a second term in the Kentucky legislature and, in fact, did not run for any elective office during the next twenty years, opting instead to remain in Grayson County to run the businesses at Falls of Rough and practice law. So at age twenty-five he left the activity of Frankfort for the solitary life of his secluded, empty home.

Lafayette's primary opportunities for fellowship coincided with his occasional trips to Louisville or other cities to attend to business. When his uncle died in 1862, his aunt returned from Texas and provided welcome company; however, her companionship could not fulfill the handsome young man's desire to share the estate of which he had recently become master and that he would one day inherit. Lafayette's brief excursions away from Falls of Rough provided him the society of several young ladies, but only one would win his heart. For her, he engaged in a persistent and passionate pursuit—a pursuit for all his dreams.

Rebecca Eleanor "Ella" Scott, circa 1860
Although family memorabilia contains photographs of all eight of
her siblings, no photograph or painting identifies Eleanor Scott.
The author believes this unmarked photograph to be that of the
young Ella.
Courtesy Mary O'Neill, Falls of Rough

Chapter Four

"Love Begat Love"

As a young man in his early twenties, Lafayette enjoyed an active social life, especially during his stays in Frankfort as a legislator. One of his fellow revelers reminded him in a March 1860 letter of the "deviltry" they had committed the previous winter and then, intimating Lafayette's continued indulgence, urged him rather facetiously to "next time to be sober enough to sign your name at the bottom of the letter." In addition, several love letters, some containing love poems, from different women indicate that Lafayette also did not lack for feminine attention. One such letter, signed "Anonymous," even exhibited a hint of jealousy when its author expressed displeasure at his visits to "'Madame' Bougers[,] Alice Smith's and others of similar character."[1]

While in the legislature and amid the social whirl of Frankfort, Lafayette may have first noticed the young lady that would eventually become his wife, but the courtship did not develop until the winter of 1864-65. The object of his attention was twenty-three year-old Rebecca Eleanor Scott, daughter of Robert Wilmot and Elizabeth Brown Scott, whose Locust Hill residence overlooked the Scott farm just five miles from Frankfort. Robert Scott, a member of Kentucky's planter aristocracy, had proved himself a leading farmer and stock breeder; his wife, Elizabeth, belonged to the famous Brown family of Frankfort. Their five daughters, of which Ella was second oldest, were leading belles in the social circles of Frankfort, where they frequented the more prominent social affairs of the city.[2]

Lafayette's ardor toward Rebecca Eleanor, called "Ella" by friends and family, became more intense in mid-March of 1865. While in Louisville, he mailed Ella his photograph, but when she did not acknowledge its receipt, he wrote to inquire and at the same time to request her photograph, closing his letter with the impersonal "Truly Yours." Then in May when he learned from Ella's brother-in-law, S. I. M. Major, that she would soon arrive in town to attend a hop, he sent a hastily written note asking her to see him just before the event; he indicated that he "had something important to say" to her. That encounter must have led to his calling at her home because a few days later, on 4 June, he wrote her from his Falls of Rough residence reminiscing about their recent visit at Locust Hill. In the letter he openly expressed his love for Ella and his hopes for the future.

While his words reveal a man already deeply in love, he clearly recognized the lack of such intensity on her part. In fact, he was so aware of her reluctance that he expressed to her a haunting fear that his "many bright hopes and high antici-pation . . . may never be realized." She offered him hope, though, by quoting "love begat love," whereupon he felt cer-tain that she would soon give him her "heart & hand" and eventually "join your fair name to mine."[3]

Lafayette attempted during the next six months to win Ella's heart completely and convince her to marry him. He filled his letters with romantic proclamations, some of which inclined toward the poetic, referring to her in such terms as "fair enchantress" and "the dearest one of earth," while also recalling the "almost ecstatic bliss enjoyed" of a Sunday afternoon visit. He obviously made progress in his quest, for by September they had discussed rather intimate topics, including Lafayette's potential as a lover, about which Ella must have expressed some doubt. He admitted his "phlegmatic temperament" and lack of an impulsive nature; however, he felt himself as capable as any other man of "loving with . . . great zeal." Ella finally acquiesced to Lafayette's proposal sometime in early 1866, probably in January or February.[4]

At that point Lafayette's letters relentlessly and almost desperately began to urge Ella to schedule a spring wedding. However, as spring became summer, he persisted in his attempts to convince her to set the earliest possible wedding date. He wrote her often and, in many cases, chided her for not responding to his letters, sometimes accusing her of indifference and at other times purporting that his letters lacked enough interest "to merit a reply."[5]

As early as Christmas 1865, when Lafayette had not received a letter from Ella in four or five weeks, he became convinced that someone was intercepting his correspondence to her. To surmount that obstacle, he went so far as to disguise his handwriting on the envelope and to mail the letter from a different post office to effect a strange postmark. Such action was probably only a ploy to shame her into being more attentive to his feelings, as he stated that he preferred to suspect sabotage rather than believe her indifferent to him. At other times he spoke of frightful dreams that caused him to worry about her welfare, resulting in his frequent admonishments to be careful for fear that all his hopes for the future would be destroyed. And because her health did seem somewhat delicate, his entreaties that she take care of herself pervaded their courtship correspondence; he wrote that he often prayed nothing would happen to her.[6]

Lafayette's pleas for a wedding date continued throughout the summer and into the fall of 1866; his future rested solely with her response because he had received permission for her "hand" shortly after she had accepted his proposal. In an early spring letter to her, Lafayette referred to a "full conference" he hoped she had held with her parents. He had seemed worried, having expressed early in their courtship that his reputation had been "most unjustly and maliciously slandered." Lafayette hoped to convince Mr. and Mrs. Scott that he had been maligned but feared they would not approve of him. However, he soon learned that her parents had endorsed their union, and about a week later he wrote them a rather formal thank-you letter in which he expressed gratitude at being welcomed into their family; he also completely assured them of Ella's protection and welfare under his "future guardianship."[7]

Eleanor Scott's childhood home, Locust Hill, near Frankfort, Kentucky
Courtesy James and Marion Ferguson, Richmond, Kentucky

Finally, in late September, Lafayette received the letter he had been awaiting. In his response to Ella, dated 1 October, he expressed his great pleasure with her decision: they would be married in nine days on 10 October. While he seemed somewhat perturbed that he had so few days in which to make the necessary preparations, he would only hint at any inconvenience by saying he was unable to give her the names of groomsmen until "quite a number" of his friends had answered his hastily written dispatches. (To her credit, her letters of 16 and 25 September had arrived together and somewhat tardy.) Within two days he had dispatched himself to the Scott home in Frankfort so that he, Ella, and her family could plan the wedding "preliminaries." Lafayette's approximate eighteen-month pursuit finally had its desired result, and his "sweet . . . thought" and "blissful . . . anticipation" became reality. On the evening of Wednesday, 10 October 1866 (Lafayette's thirty-first birthday), Lafayette Green married Rebecca Eleanor Scott in her family home at Locust Hill.[8]

Between the wedding date and the end of January 1867, Mr. and Mrs. Lafayette Green made a trip to New York. Although a lack of details about the journey prevents anything more than speculation about its nature, the proximity of the excursion to their wedding date and the fact that Ella loved to travel suggest it was a wedding trip, his gift to her. While in New York Lafayette offered to buy his bride "an elegant diamond ring," but Ella opted to be more practical and chose a piano instead. She gave two reasons: she did not feel her husband's fortune would allow spending so much on a ring, and the inhabitants of her new home community could not appreciate diamonds; in fact, she believed "they could not distinguish them from paste."[9]

Ella had only begun her life in Falls of Rough, and already her attitude toward her new home seemed fixed. She felt that the approximate one hundred miles that separated her from family and the gaieties of a capital city completely removed her from the world. Could she ever be content among people so foreign and in a location so isolated? She would certainly try to make the Falls her home because, foremost, it was her duty to her husband. But she also faced the trials of managing a household in the remote community that so distressed her. These tasks proved challenging and perhaps more difficult than she had ever imagined they could be. This place was no Locust Hill![10]

"Backwoods Country Home"

leanor Scott Green's childhood Locust Hill had domi-
nated the thoughts of Lafayette Green throughout their
courtship. Not only was it the home of the young woman he
adored, but it also loomed as a measure against which she
would judge the home he would offer her.

Lafayette had visited the Scott's stately manor house,
the only home Ella had ever known, and had no doubt grown
familiar with the beauty of its grounds, from the little pools in
the front yard and the "great variety of roses" to the expansive
fruit orchards and acres of fields beyond. Furthermore, he was
well aware of the social atmosphere it afforded her. Its location at the crossroads of two main transportation arteries provided both easy access to other destinations as well as a steady
stream of visitors, and its five-mile proximity to Frankfort
offered numerous potential entertainments, especially when
the legislature was in session. And he knew too well that Ella
enjoyed such "gaieties," as he admonished her at times during
their courtship of the effect that "nocturnal dissipations" could
have on her health.[1]

Lafayette seemed to believe that at least some of Ella's

reluctance to commit to him might concern the drastic lifestyle change she would experience after her marriage and subsequent move to Grayson County. He even expressed to her the wish that he had a more attractive home to offer, one that she was less "averse to going to." Whether she actually anticipated the full extent of the necessary adjustment and responsibility is not known.[2]

The Green manor house at Falls of Rough was quite luxurious compared to the others in the area, but it was not yet the twenty-two-room mansion it would become some fourteen years later. In fact, only after a comparison to the houses the newlywed discovered in her recreational horseback rides through the countryside did Ella realize the advantages of her own; as a result, she decided to become reconciled to her "lot."[3]

She found those neighboring houses to be lonesome-looking and their inhabitants, the farther back she went, to be "so distressingly ignorant." In a letter to her mother, not quite four months after her marriage, she described herself "situated . . . in a country inhabited by the most ignorant class of people[,] not one grain of congeniality between us[,] completely hemmed in on all sides by impassable <u>dirt</u> roads." She eventually learned to plan around the road conditions for her excursions out and guests' visits in, but she never reconciled herself with the nature of most of the inhabitants. Instead, within a few years she had determined to bring them some enlightenment, especially through education and religion.[4]

During her first months at Falls of Rough, the new Mrs. Green felt isolated in her community, but most of all she was lonely for her family and the life to which she had grown accustomed. She wondered whether her presence was "missed in the Ball room" and determined to "remind them once more" of her existence if she could leave the Falls in time to do so. She spent a great deal of time away from the Falls and with her family near Frankfort over the next few years; during her pregnancies she sometimes stayed away months at a time, causing Lafayette to express his hope on one occasion that she would soon return to their "backwoods country home." Less than three months after her wedding and at a time when Lafayette planned to be away from home on business, Ella's father urged her to visit her old Frankfort home. The invitation probably resulted from Ella's complaints to her parents, without any attempts to mask her feelings, of her boredom and discontent in her new residence. When she did remain home, Ella's parents sent her newspapers and magazines almost weekly so that she could remain in touch with "the outside world." They also were faithful correspondents. The letters of the Scott parents and their seven surviving children show them to have been a close, loving family who reciprocally offered lifelong concern and support. And Ella looked often to them for advice and succor.[5]

Ella's loneliness at the Falls intensified when her new husband had to be away overnight, even though Ann Green, the aunt who had reared Lafayette, still lived there. Ella enjoyed her aunt's company and expressed affection for "Aunt Green," speaking often in her letters to family members of their shared activities. But while her presence did not prevent Ella's loneliness, neither did it preclude her being afraid during "Mr. Green's" absences. Ella was so frightened that on one occasion she was almost too nervous to write "a very inteligible [sic] letter" to her parents in order to relate that fear. She explained: "My lonely condition has excited my imagination to such a pitch that bugaboo & blue devils are hiding in every hole & corner, the gnawing of a rat would scatter my senses to the four winds."[6]

On a different occasion she took preventive measures for protection in her new, remote location and described her "preparation for defence [sic]" in a letter to her mother, again referring to the "horror of loneliness." She explained that first, before dark, she checked every nook and corner of her bed-

room, including "under the bed, in the closets, & wardrobe .
. . then [I] bolt the shudders & lock the windows." After
those precautions she visited with her aunt until time for bed,
when she would "fly to my room, double locking the door
leaving no place for hobgoblins to enter except through the
keyhole." At this point she put "two pistols (ready for any
emergency) on the table near the bed, leaving the lamp burning all night & having the cry 'Murder Mr. Major' on the tip
of my tongue." (The murder cry reference is unclear, although
Ella did have a brother-in-law named Major whose vices produced much grief for the Scott family.) She acknowledged to
her parents that, in the light of day at least, her fears were
ungrounded, as "the people are quiet & peacible *[sic]*."[7]

"Auntie" Green had eagerly welcomed her new niece
to the Falls and probably offered the bride invaluable assistance in growing familiar with the daily operations of life
there. During Ella's absences she also provided company for
Lafayette, served as his nurse when necessary, and sometimes
oversaw the running of the household. At other times Ella was
the elder Mrs. Green's nurse, often appealing to her brother
Preston Scott, a physician in Louisville, for medical advice and
prescriptions on her aunt's behalf.[8]

But one aspect of the presence of the manor house's
former mistress grew to be a source of some difficulty for Ella.
She hinted at the problem when she reported, after five years
of marriage, that she and Auntie were getting along charm-
ingly "since I finally have control of everything." However, a
year later Ella continued to struggle with this complication,
stating that she desperately wanted "supreme control of the
kitchen."[9]

Overall, Ella appreciated her aunt's wisdom, her con-
tribution later in caring for her child, and her help with everyday tasks. When Ann Green died in 1877, Ella wrote to a sister that she had hired a governess who also "attends to the

housekeeping" as well as some sewing and other chores, "but she does not fill Aunt's place." The letter also reveals that Ella considered inviting a relative, perhaps the unmarried sister to whom she was writing, to the Falls to help fill her aunt's void, but she acknowledged that none of her family would ever be content there "with such surroundings"; she even doubted that she, herself, would ever be.[10]

Although servants completed many of the chores required for a well-run household, keeping good servants who were cooperative and efficient posed another obstacle for the mistress; cooks seemed to offer the greatest problem. Early in her role as hostess, Ella complained of her servant's skills after she had entertained one of Lafayette's cousins reputed to be a fine housekeeper. She hoped her fine table presentation of silver and china had compensated for any lack in the food. The cook responsible for these misgivings was the first Ella hired after the Green's long-time cook, a freed slave named America, left the Falls in 1870. Over the next few years both Ella and Lafayette searched for and hired at least four other cooks to replace the previous ones, who either quit or were dismissed. Sometimes their capable servants were quarrelsome, and on at least one occasion the dissolution of a dispute required Lafayette's intervention with a threat of dismissal. A servant's fear of being sent away from the Green home usually effected improved behavior.[11]

The general unrest of servants, both household as well as field workers, was a pervasive concern on the Green property, particularly between 1869 and the early 1870s. The year 1870 seems to have been one of especial unrest, for Lafayette was disturbed about how many of the hired help would remain. At the beginning of that year, he was so uncertain of the number that he requested the help of his brother-in-law in Louisville, Preston Scott, in seeking "negro men without families as well as women" for employment. Seven months later, with the harvest approaching, Lafayette had to stay in the fields because his "field servants" refused to work under the supervision of their overseer and then quit in the busiest season when the crops had produced more abundantly than usual. Two years later found Lafayette again negotiating with his tenants and laborers, with all except his best Negro man agreeing to remain.[12]

Such worry and tedious handling of personalities only added to the fatigue of a farmer also involved in several other enterprises. So to alleviate some of his anxiety about an adequate work force, Lafayette built extra tenant housing. By early 1883 Lafayette had completed several comfortable houses on the property, prompting Ella to boast to her parents that "with so many new buildings & attractive cottages our little village is to be quite proud of."[13]

Although the house servants frequently posed problems, Ella generally had the number, if not the quality, she required. In fact, in 1871 she complained, though mildly, that she had such an abundance of servants indoors that they prevented her receiving adequate exercise. However, she gladly resorted to horseback rides to provide the needed activity. At other times the daily operations of her home offered plenty to keep her occupied, particularly supervising the procurement, preservation, and preparation of food for her growing family.[14]

The Green family generally enjoyed a variety of foods, especially meats, for the farm produced cattle, sheep, goats, and hogs, with products of the latter filling a large portion of the meat house. In November of 1887, Lafayette butchered thirty-five hogs and produced, among other foodstuffs, lard, sausage, and spareribs; pork was so plentiful that year that Lafayette supposed the family would eat it instead of turkey for Thanksgiving. Hog-killing one year produced approximately one hundred hams, and sending some of these to family members, especially Ella's parents in Frankfort, was not an unusual practice. In addition, if one or more of the Green children were boarding away from home at the time of hog-killing, they could expect a package of freshly processed meat, along with other farm-fresh products like eggs, butter, and flour and meal ground at the family mill. On one occasion the Greens sent some sausage to one of the children in Louisville with the instruction that it be sold "at 20¢ per lb." That same child, at home a few years earlier and a benefactor of the day's activities, described the family's evening meal to a brother away from home: "We just finished hog killing and had a pig tail dinner." The Greens sometimes, if not always, locked the meat house and carefully guarded the keys.[15]

The only meat Ella wished for but could not provide for her table when she first moved to the Falls was fowl, the mink population's being too big a threat without the protection of a henhouse. But thanks to the neighbors' habit of exchanging chickens and eggs for the dry goods they bought at the general store, Ella generally did not lack for either. However, she wanted to raise her own chickens, preferring Plymouth Rock hens, and within a few years she had her henhouse as well as her hens and chicks; later she also raised

Catfish from the millpond (fishermen unidentified), circa 1900
Courtesy Mary O'Neill, Falls of Rough

turkeys. To add to the variety of meats, the hills and woods were full of game and, because Lafayette was too busy to go hunting, he made a deal with "a fine hunter," agreeing to "supply the shot" in exchange for "half the kill." Rabbits must have been a dining speciality, for guests acclaimed Ella's "rabbits with real cream gravy." Fish, too, were plentiful and conveniently available with the river located just a few hundred yards from the house; in fact, the millpond held a reputation for yielding great bounties of large fish, especially catfish.[16]

Most other items on the menu came from the garden, a project Ella eagerly anticipated. One of the endeavors she seemed eager to begin each spring was preparing hot beds for the early planting of lettuce. Although she probably could have left such tasks entirely to the servants, her belief that "idleness is the king of all evils," as well as her enjoyment of the out-of-doors, compelled her to keep busy.[17]

During the first several years of her marriage, when she spent much of her time away from the Falls, either Aunt Green or one of Lafayette's grown nieces, specifically Jennie Short, carried out the necessary tasks of gardening or "putting by" garden products, often at Ella's direction. In addition to lettuce, the products of Ella's garden not only included the standard garden vegetables but also raspberries and flowers. Most of the fruits and vegetables were canned or preserved in some form, as guests sometimes left with gifts of pickles or jam.[18]

The surrounding woods also augmented the garden's bounty by yielding hickory nuts, chestnuts, and blackberries. And many fruits not native to Kentucky were available first from Ella's parents' Florida farm and later from the Greens' farm there. So between November and March, when Mr. and Mrs. Scott were in their "temporary southern home," the Green family enjoyed rather frequent shipments of oranges, grapefruits, lemons, and limes, particularly around the

Christmas holidays. In return, Ella sometimes sent her wintering parents maple sugar. And if the winter vegetables that filled the cellar did not satisfy the pre- or post-season palate, family members who happened to be passing through Louisville sometimes filled "orders" for fresh vegetables available at the larger markets there. After one business trip to Owensboro, Lafayette and Ella themselves returned with a sixty-pound watermelon and a large bunch of bananas. The provisions for a varied and flavorful diet never seemed lacking at the Falls.[19]

Family fare varied by season, but fresh corn sometimes meant "a nice corn pudding every morning for breakfast," accompanied at times by fresh "tomatos*[sic]* with plenty of onions." In the mid-1880s Ella found that her ailing stomach permitted an appetite for only "jole*[sic]* & greens," a common item on a farm menu. Sunday dinner for them, as for many country people, was probably special, and one such bill of fare consisted of "vegetable soup, saddle of mutton & vegetables & stewed pears & cake." As early as the 1870s, Ella had indicated that she and Aunt Green "eat like birds." Though Ella suffered all her life with digestive problems, a healthy appetite never seemed a problem for the other members of the family.[20]

For food preparation the Green household generally relied upon the cook, although occasionally Ella had to help an inexperienced or overworked one. For example, in 1887 the Green's seven and a half-year-old daughter brought home from church "a raft of children," and Ella had to help "in getting up a good dinner." Meal preparation became more of a task as the Green children grew in number (to four) and in size, for with age came visiting friends and relatives (usually cousins) and the young children's governess or teacher, who boarded with the family. In the mid-1880s Ella wrote her mother that she was keeping busy with her large family, especially feeding them: "six men, three children & Miss Cummings [the governess]." (She did not account for the large number of men.)[21]

Not a food item but nonetheless important to the Greens' dining was ice. And just as hog-killing was a winter ritual at the Falls, so was "putting up" ice. The Greens had only one ice house, located a few yards behind the general store, although they considered building a second to prevent their "begging neighbors" from depleting their supply. In January 1884 filling the ice house required ten workmen several hours just to saw ice from the river; then the ice blocks still needed to be moved, stacked, and covered with sawdust. This particular year the ice was thicker than usual and Ed Moorman, the farm manager who oversaw the project, had to borrow a larger saw to complete the task. When he finished, he reported to Lafayette that the ice was "splendid." Once the ice house was again full, the Greens referred to the completed project with pride as well as a sense of relief and feeling of security. In the winter of 1892, filling the ice house became somewhat more important because the previous summer Lafayette had agreed to supply ice for a branch train of the Louisville, St Louis and Texas Railway Company.[22]

Another of Ella's household responsibilities was as hostess to the numerous visitors at the Green manor. Almost from the time of her arrival at Falls of Rough, she entertained guests, many of them relatives visiting Aunt Green, often for extended periods. Lafayette, too, enjoyed inviting "surprise" guests, usually businessmen or farmers from outside the community who happened to be working with him at mealtime. So Ella probably grew accustomed to accommodating visitors, although not always under the most convenient circumstances for her.[23]

By the early 1890s Ella began to entertain more often according to her own designs, frequently inviting friends, relatives, and acquaintances to dinner or to spend a few days in her home. Consequently, the demands upon the cook—and the ingredients with which she worked—became ever more important, and the Greens established an acclaimed reputation for all their amenities, including their "elaborate table." Family friend J. Fry Lawrence of Louisville looked forward in January 1893 to a few days' visit to the Falls for "inhaling the pure country air." And although he requested that Ella not go to extra trouble but treat him and his accompanying daughter "as home folks," he spoke of "the long and well filled dining room" as an anticipated attraction.[24]

Before Lawrence planned his trip, he asked Ella to "say if your house is full, as usual," for he and his daughter Mary were just two of the Greens' many guests between 1891 and 1895. Perhaps Lawrence's characterization of the household to which he eagerly anticipated a visit helps explain why the Green home was so often filled with visitors during this period:

> The gay light of the library, . . . the chat
> of the boys, the Solomon remarks of the Senator,
> the bright flashes from Willis [then age 23], the
> good old tunes on the piano, the cherry cheeks
> and lips of Jennie [age 13], the melting glances of
> the pretty teacher, the cute sayings of Robert [age
> 10], and last tho not least, the entertaining,
> witty, agreeable, and sometimes caustic conversa-
> tion of "My Lady Green."[25]

Otherwise, the question concerning why this period shows evidence of such an increased number of guests is open to speculation. Perhaps the children's ages (the youngest was almost eight and a half years old in early 1891) allowed their mother more time and freedom. Quite possibly the increase was the result of a lifetime accumulation of business and political acquaintances; in addition, the railroad had come to the Falls in 1890, thereby diminishing the isolation that characterized its location. Or maybe Ella had finally embraced her backwoods home now that she had made it her own, in part at least, by having the house remodeled to her specifications, which included increasing its size to twenty-two rooms. It had become more similar to her Locust Hill home and was capable of comfortably accommodating several guests. Probably a combination of these factors provides the explanation, but the beauty of their home afforded both Ella and Lafayette great pride and surely intensified their desire to receive guests.

When the young bride first arrived at her new home at the Falls in October 1866, she had had to see the poor state of her neighbors' homes before she could appreciate her own, which she naturally compared to her Locust Hill dwelling. And from the beginning Ella had her plans for what her county home would physically become. In November 1867 she looked forward to getting her "place . . . in trim, apple pie order" and hoped her husband's new or improved "sawmill to work wonders in the way of improvements." She suggested Lafayette's recognition of and corroboration with her plans when she reported, "Mr. Green says all of my air castles are now built from planks and lumber sawed at his mill, a new hen house is one of them." Obviously, the house and grounds in 1866 did not possess the grandeur of later years, after the Greens added numerous tenant houses and outbuildings and extensively renovated the manor house.[26]

A description of the house to which Ella moved in 1866, the one built by Willis Green in the 1830s, is unavailable. However, young Lafayette had been concerned that this house would not please the young lady from Frankfort. Some of his worry might have been justified, for in one of Ella's extensive absences (mid-September 1869 through March/April 1870) he attempted to make the house more cold-weather comfortable by having the chimneys topped, some grates reset, and their bedroom grate enlarged. Even with those improvements, keeping the house warm proved quite a task. Ella complained of her difficulty in the cold January of 1884, saying that she spent all of her time "trying

The Greens (and an unidentified lady) pose before their home, Falls of Rough. (L-R) Unidentified lady, Lafayette Green, Jennie, Willis, Eleanor, Robert, and Preston, circa 1894 Courtesy Mary O'Neill, Falls of Rough

to keep the fires burning" and adding, "all the water in the house is frozen." The water to which she referred came from a cistern; but when rain failed to provide the needed supply, the source was a nearby spring.[27]

In 1877, when Ella anticipated a visit from her parents, she had the parlor made into a bedroom so that they could be more comfortable. This necessity might indicate that either the house still did not have adequate guest accommodations or that the remodeling process was in progress. By 1880, three years later, the house had been sufficiently changed to warrant the New York Continental Insurance Company's requiring that a new policy be written. Little evidence of the full extent of the changes to the house remain, but a receipt dated 19 August 1879 shows that Lafayette received sixteen air grates from a Louisville iron works company. The need for these grates, to be installed in the foundation masonry, suggests some renovation as well as considerable enlargement to the structure.[28]

By the fall of 1880 Ella was involved in decorating or redecorating, for she received a new carpet, delivered by the local lady who had finished it. The following spring she inquired to John Shillito & Co. of Cincinnati about window shade prices and samples, and then only six years later workmen installed parquetry in the dining room. When the carpenters finished and she had waxed the new hardwood floor, Ella marveled at its splendor, which remains evident more than one hundred years later. Made of walnut and ash, it is laid in a checkerboard design except for a large bordered rectangle, presumably the area covered by a carpet where the dining table sat. The entire front portion of the house—foyer, parlor, and hall—has the same beautiful flooring, some of which is arranged in a herringbone pattern.[29]

The flooring is not the only masterpiece which survives today in the Green "mansion." The chestnut, cherry, and walnut woodwork—doors and door facings, window facings, wainscoting, broad winding staircase, and foyer arch—testifies to the quality of the interior materials and workmanship. And although the white-painted brick exterior shows the wear of time, the building, Italianate in design with a bit of New Orleans flavor in the wrought iron trim of the front porch, remains structurally sound. Excepting the natural ravages of the elements, it sits today just as it sat for the mid-1890s photograph of Mr. and Mrs. Lafayette Green and family—in quiet, stately elegance.

The impressive structure was not one of ostentation, but a nurturing home, much lived in and enjoyed, for the third generation of Greens. It was, actually, the only home that generation would ever know. And not long after Lafayette and Ella's union, their thoughts had turned to that family—their hopes for a fulfilled future and an assurance of posterity.

Foyer of the Green home, circa 1963
Courtesy Louisville Courier-Journal Magazine, Louisville, Kentucky

Chapter Six

"Quite Large Under the Apron"

Lafayette and Ella wasted little time starting a family; approximately seven months after the October wedding Ella miscarried their first child. She had either anticipated problems or had taken advantage of her condition to escape her loneliness and homesickness, for by late March 1867 she was at her parents' home near Frankfort; from there she had easier access to the expertise of her brother, Dr. Preston Scott of Louisville. Lafayette remained at the Falls but wrote to her often, lamenting her absence. On 5 May 1867 Ella's father, Robert Wilmot Scott, wrote to Lafayette with the sad and shocking news that, despite all efforts to save it, "the baby was aborted." But at age twenty-six Ella recovered quickly and by the end of the year was again pregnant.[1]

Once more Ella, proud of her "enlarged state," left the Falls so that she could be near her brother in time for the delivery. Due to give birth in September, she traveled to Louisville the first part of July and from there to Locust Hill to remain until she and the expected baby were capable of the trip home, four to five months later. In mid-August Lafayette planned a trip to Frankfort for a visit with his wife, and although sickness delayed his travel, he recovered sufficiently to carry out his plans soon thereafter. In a letter to her from the Falls dated 17 September, he remarked that by then she must be "quite large under the apron." Ten days later, on 27 September 1868, Ella gave birth to a daughter, and by 3 October Lafayette had received news of the birth and well-being of both mother and child, whereupon he agreed with the name *Elizabeth* (Ella's mother's name) but suggested, if not that, *Mary*. He immediately made preparations to travel to Frankfort within the next week or so to see his wife and newborn daughter.[2]

Elizabeth, "Lizzie" to her father, was home with her mother by December but had begun to lose weight by early May, at the age of eight months; she did not seem sick otherwise, however. Scott family members wrote letters of concern and offered their varied diagnoses for the baby's weight loss, but Ella's milk was the most often-mentioned culprit. Ella's sister-in-law, Mrs. John Orlando Scott of Owensboro, who herself had a healthy seven-month-old son, offered to share her milk with little Elizabeth if it would help. However, no measures could save her, and Elizabeth died on 28 September 1869, the day after her first birthday. Correspondence between Ella and Lafayette indicates that the day after the baby's death Ella was at her brother's house in Louisville, probably where the baby had died after attempts by Dr. Scott to save her.[3]

Even as they buried their first child, the Greens were expecting their second; Ella was almost six months pregnant. By October she had already decided to spend the winter at Locust Hill to await the birth, her fear of some complication probably heightened by the earlier losses. So again Lafayette, "Auntie" Green, and their Falls of Rough home were without their lady's "sweet countenance" as Ella sought the support and solace of her family. Ella's sister, Louise Wing of

Owensboro, regretted that she had never seen baby Elizabeth but promised to visit with Ella in Frankfort and "help you make all kinds of pretty things for your comforting hopes in November." Ella's brother Preston, however, urged her in mid-November to stay with him in Louisville; he cited several reasons she should do so in an appeal that left her little choice.[4]

Although her departure date is uncertain, Ella did give birth in Louisville on 4 January 1870, and Lafayette soon received news that after much suffering Ella had produced a son and both were doing well. Mother and baby Willis, named for his paternal great-uncle, remained in Louisville through February and by mid-March had returned to

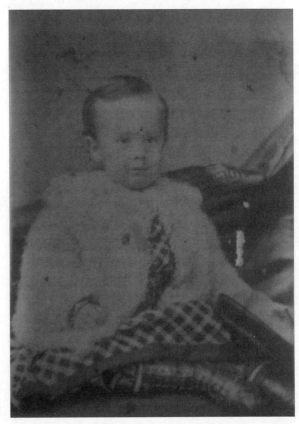

Willis Green,
circa 1872
Courtesy
Mary O'Neill,
Falls of Rough

Frankfort. Shortly thereafter the family was together at Falls of Rough.[5]

By early August Ella had grown "uneasy about Willis," who was losing weight and covered with "eruptions" that itched and prevented his sleeping. Plans were in the making for a trip to the spa at Grayson Springs, twenty miles away, where she hoped the sulfur water would effect a cure. The local physician, Dr. Mosely, had diagnosed the problem as the "itch" and prescribed opiates. However, Ella learned soon afterwards that her servant Mary had contracted poison oak and spread it to the family; even she and Lafayette were infected. This time her eight-month-old recovered quickly and continued to thrive.[6]

Two months later Willis was cutting teeth and interrupting the family's sleep, sleep that his father and mother needed badly. Lafayette spent long days cutting corn with his "ten or fifteen hands," and Ella arose "every morning at four o'clock" to "have his breakfast prepared before daylight." Obviously Willis' crying caused a dire lack of rest; Ella reported that she had to "jog" Lafayette on both sides "to get him wide enough awake to dress for breakfast." Once awake, Lafayette then experienced some stiffness and brief difficulty walking. Still not content with her life in the country, Ella took advantage of her husband's infirmity to propose the family's relocation to a more favorable climate. However, she concluded from Lafayette's reaction that he was really attached to "this sink hole."[7]

Not only did Willis thrive, but his mother's love for him flourished as well. She described her one-year-old to her parents as "a bright, cheery, fat little pig" who "is par excellence, beats all the other grandchildren put together." She further related, "He is a great abolitionist in practice, kisses and hugs all the negroes on the place and infinitely prefers them to any of us." Willis' continued well-being helped produce at least some decrease in Ella's discontent. A letter of this period

contains one of the few documented expressions of her affection for Lafayette; she described herself "content," due in part
to "the kind thoughtful attentions of the next best husband in
the world" who, with age, might "rank 'first best.'" Ella's
endearing allusion to her father exemplified the strong ties she
held to her family; although happier than before, she still felt
that they were too far, over bad and sometimes impassable
roads, from her isolated Grayson County home.[8]

At two years old Willis showed an interest in "farm
play," much to his mother's chagrin. She already hoped he
would not choose farming as a career because of the long, hard
work it required, as her husband's constant fatigue attested.
Some of Willis' play involved building a "corn cob pen" and
filling it with stick pigs. He also made a game of waiting for
the local hunter who supplied the family with wild game.
When the youngster spotted the man returning with his
bounty, he sang a special song and successfully insisted upon a
bird to pluck.[9]

While Ella and Lafayette enjoyed the antics of their
toddler and the liveliness he afforded their otherwise quiet
home, Ella again became pregnant. By June of 1873 she was
once more considering accepting her brother's invitation to his
Louisville home, especially since she had absolutely no confidence in the local doctor, whose misdiagnosis of something as
simple as poison oak had solidified Ella's distrust and disgust;
she refused to be "treated by this drunken, opium-eating ignorant Dr." She also was concerned not to "run any risk this
month so that I may not be so unfortunate as heretofore" and
credited her brother with having saved Willis' life four years
before.[10]

Once again Mr. and Mrs. Green had reason to be worried about their unborn child. Before Ella left for Louisville,
planning as before to remain for the birth and recovery, her
mother traveled to Grayson County for a brief visit with her

daughter's family. By 20 June she must have been with the Greens for quite some time and somewhat longer than the visit had been planned. Mr. Scott wrote to his wife that he had gone to the train station three times to pick her up and was perplexed each time that she had not arrived. However, he had finally received her three letters informing him of Ella's sad situation, whereupon he declared his wife's visit not only timely but "Providentially directed." Ella had lost another child.[11]

Little Willis continued to thrive on his farm-fresh diet, especially milk, and Lafayette was often away from home, sometimes in Evansville, Indiana, trying to sell the lumber from his sawmill. Although Ella complained of her "widowhood," she again became pregnant and in September of 1874 lost yet another baby girl. Shortly after the "misfortune," during October, Ella took Willis with her to visit Preston in Louisville, perhaps to allow her brother to assess her health, and then on to enjoy an extended visit with her family near Frankfort. She had not yet returned to her Falls home by the end of January of 1875, and records fail to relate just how long she remained away.[12]

Meanwhile, the only companions Lafayette enjoyed at his home were Aunt Green and three other friends or relatives also living there: Mrs. Owen, Ann Green's sister; Fannie, probably Ann Green's niece; and Jennie Short, Lafayette's eighteen-year-old niece from Rumsey. Jennie was more or less overseeing the tasks of the household in Ella's absence, and Ann Green, admittedly missing the accustomed bustle and Ella and Willis' companionship, kept busy knitting, sewing, and embroidering. According to Ann, Fannie had been able to do enough spinning each day to keep them in yarn, allowing her to "knit dear Willis a pair of stockings." And before Ella returned, Lafayette was also away from the Falls for six weeks, perhaps part of which he spent with his wife and son in Frankfort. So by January, Aunt Green was lonely and longed for her family's speedy return; but she yearned especially to see Willis, who won his elders' hearts with "his bright looks and smart speeches." She welcomed Ella and Master Willis home and spent much time in his company.[13]

Ann Green had experienced poor health for some time, but details surrounding her worsening condition and death are absent. She died on 15 March 1877 and was buried beside her husband in Cave Hill Cemetery in Louisville. Though somewhat incapacitated by age and health, Auntie had been of great help in looking after young Willis. Ella needed to replace her assistance and by 24 April 1877 had hired a governess for seven-year-old Willis, whom his mother described as "fat & rosey & speckled faced."[14]

Ella was additionally concerned that Willis should have suitable playmates and did not believe the rough, illiterate neighborhood boys to be "fit companions." She appealed to relatives and acquaintances in hopes that their sons could spend the summer at the Falls. She already expected Willis Short, the teen-age son of Lafayette's sister, Elizabeth, from Rumsey; he liked to fish, boat, and horseback ride and perhaps would offer some company for Willis. But unless she could recruit some playmates and until the second Willis arrived, Master Green was left primarily to either his solitary entertainment or to diversions with the governess's daughter, with whom he played dolls and "robbed his mother's ragbag." He also sometimes "worked" in his father's tobacco warehouse prizing tobacco, where he earned ten cents for each evening's work. Ella found companions and caretakers for Willis particularly helpful this summer, for she was expecting another child in July.[15]

Ella had planned to spend the entire previous winter, 1876-77, in Louisville, having gone so far as to send her packed trunks to Caneyville, where she would board the train. However, after six weeks of obstacles in going (perhaps Aunt Green's declining health had been one deterrent), she directed the trunks' return; then following Aunt's death the roads had not been conducive to easy transportation. In addition, she had decided that she could not bear to leave her husband alone for an "indefinite time." Months afterward, however, Ella admitted feeling "like a prisoner bound to the stake" and remained discontent in her country home, "even with the best of husbands, dearest of boys, and [being the] monarch of all I survey"; she believed her life should be more useful. For some reason, she also felt she would soon die and urged her family to visit before the summer's end.[16]

Unlike her previous pregnancies and deliveries, Ella seems to have experienced no complications, and a second son, Preston Scott, was born on 17 July 1877. Two months

Preston Green (right), circa 1883 Courtesy James and Marion Ferguson, Richmond, Kentucky

later Lafayette made a trip to Chicago, presumably on business, but Ella remained at the Falls; she planned an "escape," however brief, by boat to Rumsey the following spring. She would take ten-month-old Preston so that his relatives there, the Shorts (Lafayette's sister's family), could see him before he grew out of his "babyhood." Jennie Short, then twenty-two years old, was especially close to her Uncle Lafayette's family and eager to see Preston before his mother put him in "short dresses."[17]

By the time Preston was eighteen months old, Lafayette and Ella were expecting another child, and Lafayette must have been especially pleased when on 26 September 1879 Jennie Scott was born. His posterity was already assured with two sons, and finally he had a daughter to complete his family. Perhaps this birth was even more special since his first-

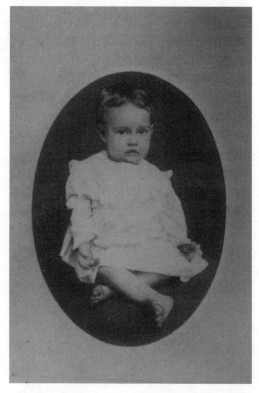

Jennie Green,
circa 1881
Courtesy Green Farms
Papers, University of
Louisville

born daughter, Elizabeth, had died the day after her first birth-day and another daughter had been stillborn. Lafayette devot-ed considerable attention to this daughter, at times doting on her. Jennie was obviously aware early of her father's adoration because at age three and a half, when her mother scolded and threatened to slap her if she did not stop kissing and teasing a sibling, the little girl replied, "Now Mama you wouldn't hit Papa's darling pet daughter when shes *[sic]* sick."[18]

All three children were thriving as 1880 arrived, and the Greens were expanding their house to accommodate the growing family. Ella still visited her Frankfort home, though the visits were generally not the extended ones of earlier years. In October 1880 she took three-year-old Preston and one-year-old Jennie with her for a visit to Locust Hill; Willis,

Willis Green,
circa 1878
Courtesy Green
Farms Papers,
University of Louisville

almost eleven, stayed home with his father, who spent most of his time tending to business in the general store. Lafayette made sure Ella knew that Willis was "doing splendidly & . . . studying well," reporting that he read until ten o'clock every night in his parents' upstairs bedroom; he had almost completed reading *Swiss Family Robinson.*[19]

In the summer of 1881, Willis underwent an operation, though details surrounding the procedure are lacking. However, he lost an eye during his youth, and the possibility exists that this surgery was the result of that loss. Only oral community recollections offer the circumstances of the incident: Willis was playing with boys shooting a bow and arrow when an arrow struck him in the eye. Young Willis spent at least part of that summer in Frankfort with his grandparents; perhaps he remained for post-operative care in the Louisville/Frankfort area, probably the site of the surgery.[20]

Willis returned to the Falls the first of September and wrote three weeks later to thank his grandfather and Aunt Etta (Henrietta Scott), who still lived with her parents, for his pleasant visit. He also told them that he was "clerking in the store" and had "a bracket saw which has an anvil, vice, drill, turning lathe and saw." He continued with hopes that his grandparents would "enjoy the golden wedding," a reference to their fiftieth wedding anniversary celebration planned for October. His letter shows careful attention to proper penmanship, neatness, and spelling; while the eleven-year-old had corrected some simple misspellings, some remained. The letter is a reflection of Willis, the student—of etiquette as well as grammatical mechanics—, and Willis, the dutiful grandson and nephew.[21]

During the period of Willis' convalescence, two-year-old Jennie was ill. Ella's sister, Mary Major of Frankfort, speculated the trouble as malaria and suggested Ella take her "up home," where Ella already planned a visit for the October anniversary celebration. Mary urged her to let Preston examine the child in Louisville on their way to Frankfort. No records indicate whether Ella heeded her sister's advice or what actually was the nature of Jennie's malady, but she recovered and nothing sinister befell the little girl, described by her relatives as "such a little darling . . . good & beautiful." Within a few months her grandmother identified the almost three-year-old as "the sweetest of them all."[22]

The next year, 1882, began with everyone seemingly healthy—Willis turned twelve and was adjusting to an artificial eye; Preston, described as "stout," seemed somewhat safe from the feared diseases, and Jennie, now twenty-eight months old, thrived under the attention of her doting father. And Ella and Lafayette awaited the birth of a fourth child.[23]

Ella, now forty years old, must have felt the impending birth would involve no complications, for she remained at the Falls. A letter from her father on 7 August did not mention the impending event and seemed instead rather business-like in content. He did express hopes that Ella could soon bring all the children to Locust Hill to visit him, as he was unable to make the trip west to see them. Approximately three weeks later, on 30 August 1882, Robert Wilmot Scott Green was born. Ella had given her father a namesake.[24]

Though Jennie was the light of her father's eye, baby Robert soon managed to equal, perhaps even surpass, the amount of attention his sister attracted from her father. Ella wrote her oldest son, away at school: "Papa said . . . that he believed Robert loved him more than any of the other children ever did, but the reason of that is the *[sic]* he pets him more." She added that Lafayette would even put down the *Louisville Courier-Journal* to pick up the baby.[25]

During most of Robert's infancy Lafayette was away from home—either in Frankfort while the Kentucky legislature was in session, in the county seat of Leitchfield some thirty miles away where Lawyer Green presented his cases in

court, or on business trips related to one of his several enterprises. Perhaps these absences made more intense the fifty-
year-old father's appreciation for his home and encouraged
more demonstrative love for his family. By the time Robert
was almost four years old, his mother described him as
extremely spoiled; when she slapped him for some infraction,
he was "so astonished he forgot to cry." However, she proud-
ly reported that he also loved to go to church and sing and that
he always said prayer at the table. Ella prophesied that he
would be her "little preacher."[26]

As the Green children matured, their mother developed special concerns about their education and training. An
avid reader herself, Ella encouraged their reading and wanted
them to have access to
good books. After her
father died in 1884, she
urged her husband to
purchase her father's
library for the benefits it
would offer the children.
Both she and Lafayette
spent hours reading to
them, sometimes even
until she grew hoarse.[27]

Ella also spent a
great deal of time and
effort hiring teachers,
who boarded and taught
in the Green home; in
some cases an additional
teacher also taught in a
schoolhouse nearby. At
different times between
1887 and 1891, at least

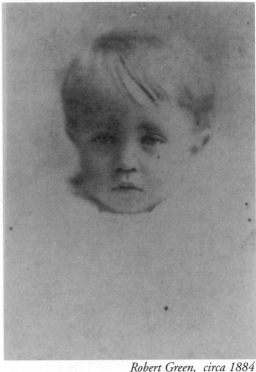

Robert Green, circa 1884
Courtesy Green Farms Papers,
University of Louisville

four different teachers taught at the Falls. One of those was Ella's twenty-one year-old niece, Louise, daughter of John Orlando Scott. The woman hired in 1891, Mary E. Thomas, received twenty dollars per month plus board and washing; she earned an additional ten dollars per month if the hotel manager charged his children to her tutelage. Sometimes the teacher undertook additional obligations; one, for example, did the family sewing in exchange for using Ella's sewing machine for her personal sewing needs.[28]

At times, perhaps when Ella could not retain or find an acceptable teacher, correspondence suggests that she might have considered sending a child to stay with friends or family in Louisville so that he or she could attend "a good school." But the children learned well under their grammar school instructors, although young Preston dreaded the idea of going to school and Robert was also a somewhat reluctant student; young Willis proved an all-around scholar and nine-year-old Jennie especially liked arithmetic. The efforts on behalf of the children's scholarly achievement paid off, for all four acquired sound educations.[29]

Just as important to their mother as their intellectual growth was the moral development of the Green children. In addition to her parental guidance, Ella felt the religious influence an important one—and not just for her children, but for the whole community. So she expended great effort in acquiring a preacher, organizing a Sunday school, encouraging the building of a church house and parsonage, and raising funds for a church organ, which she played. Sometimes when the preacher showed up late or not at all, Ella expressed concern that the children of the community would grow up to be heathens. To encourage these children to study, she gave the Sunday school twelve Bibles "so they could learn the 10 commandments," promising her class a Christmas tree if they learned them.[30]

While the children's religious habits comprised her primary interest, Ella also worried about others' souls, particularly that of her husband, and she joined other churchgoers in praying for his conversion. In October of 1887 she wrote to Willis (at Centre College) that Lafayette seemed interested and she hoped he would join the church; several letters later she happily informed her eldest son that she had "gone forward" with his father, at last a church member. During this same period Ella wrote that she had cooked all day on Friday so that she could go to church twice on Saturday, when the minister preached for four hours and then another hour by lamplight. She expressed hopes that the people would repent and related with chagrin that the collection to help pay the parsonage carpenter had netted only eight dollars.[31]

The Greens had built a Methodist church on the premises by the end of 1886 and completed the parsonage, with some community contributions, by the end of the next year. Although Ella was especially charitable in matters relating to the church, she grew weary of the habits of the parsonage carpenter, who boarded in her home. She wrote that she was tired of his "pipe & dirty room," and indicated she felt "rebellion against these sanctified members that they are not willing to help in any way." In addition, Ella had to pay for much of the church organ; she complained that she had to give ten extra dollars above the amount she had already donated because "every young man refused to give a nickel & it was so hard to think that it is hard to live in such a pig headed community." She wondered, "How can they expect favors from God when they do so little in building up his word?"[32]

Ella continued all her life to be involved in the church, conducting such activities as decorating it with paper flowers one Easter, when she reported seventy-five in Sunday school. For the same occasion she organized "a procession to march around the aisles twice & then kneel around the alter while we

sang Christ Arose" as well as a short drama involving costumes
and a flower-covered cross. By undertaking these kinds of
projects, she not only celebrated her beliefs in the customs of
her upbringing, but she also exposed her neighbors to beautiful and dignified ceremonies which many might never have
witnessed otherwise.[33]

Although she continued to express displeasure about
life in such a remote area and to experience difficulty in under-
standing her neighbors' lifestyles, Ella seemed to define her
role among them as that of benefactor and edifier, with the
church providing the primary means for that role. Just as she
urged her eldest son to serve as a good example for his younger
siblings, she felt she should be a model of the Christian principles she espoused.

Ella helped her community by sharing her family's
means as well as her personal service and time. When a lady
in a remote part of the community wrote Ella that she needed
a pair of shoes so that she could attend church, Ella sent the
letter to the general store with her own note directing her husband to attend to the delivery of the shoes. At another time,
when many children of the area were ill and dying, Ella devot-
ed so much of her energy to their care that she grew thinner
than ever before—so thin that she warned her parents of her
appearance before she paid them a visit. And a year later, as
Ella lay very ill, a correspondent recalled how kind she was "to
everybody, especially the poor and needy." So although she
never really fit inside the social structure of her neighbors, Ella
did find her niche among them—as a friend in times of
need.[34]

Ella filled well the role of nursemaid, in part because
she was kind and unafraid of hard work; she also possessed a
buoyant personality. An acquaintance reflected upon a time
when she had received Ella's solace and recalled her "cheerful
face & and merry laugh— . . . tender heart— . . . words of
comfort— . . . hospitality." A close friend, feeling somewhat

depressed, wrote that nothing would keep her "zest up" like seeing Ella. Another acquaintance typified Ella, about fifty years old, as having "more life than half the young girls."[35]

The same vivacity and fun-loving nature that cheered the sick and impressed her acquaintances yielded numerous activities to enliven the community and especially the Green household. On the expansive grounds of their Falls of Rough home, the members of the Green family and their guests discovered abundant entertainment. But that which was not naturally available was easily designed and executed under the direction of the lively lady of the house. Amusement comprised an integral part of her life, and her ebullient spirit was evident in the good times at the Falls.

Chapter Seven

"Fun at the Falls"

Ella and Lafayette Green's Falls home was renowned for its gay times. Not only did family and guests revel in the spacious mansion and its expansive river-enhanced grounds, but they also enjoyed pageants, plays, and parties filled with music and games. The Greens' reputation as superb hosts to both young and old only increased the appeal of their hospitable residence.

The Green home always seemed a special place for children, one that considered play an important part of their discovery and learning. Consequently, the children of friends, neighbors, and family frequently "collected" there to delight in the rather lenient structure that governed their amusement. Ella wrote to Willis in 1883 that "pandemonium has let loose when all the children are in the sitting room playing, just now there are eight in all sizes, colors & ages in there kicking up the dust & getting ready for their tea party." Only three of those children were her own. Such a scene was repeated many times over and even continued, with increasingly mature activities, through the period of the young Greens' courtship

78

days, when Falls of Rough was reportedly a "meeting place" for young men and women.[1]

Horseback riding was a favorite form of entertainment and exercise for both Ella and the children, who also liked to ride the Shetland ponies Lafayette raised. But the river provided much of the children's amusement. In addition to the usual fishing, boating, and swimming, the river's bank offered its own prizes. On one occasion Robert, about five years old, and some playmates brought a huge bullfrog into the parlor, inducing an indulgent Ella only to exclaim that her "head swims after looking at such an ugly beast." And the river fun was not limited to warm weather. In February of 1896, eighteen-year-old Preston wrote his sister from college that he had been home and skated on the river all weekend; he described the "ice like glass," adding "you could skate for miles and miles."[2]

Guests wrote frequently to thank the Greens for entertaining visits, often referring to their enjoyment of the piano's dulcet refrains. As a young girl Ella had studied music and excelled at the instrument; her mother wrote that her daughter would "play three hours if she is not interrupted by company." That love and talent for playing was a significant element in the Green home, where visitors often arrived just to hear Ella play; one evening she played for such guests until her back ached. And among her repertoire were polkas, whose liveliness invited dancing. The Greens also liked to engage guests in card games, whist and euchre being favorites.[3]

Occasionally theme parties and stage "productions" provided amusement, especially in the case of "an old fashion 'masquerade breakdown.'" The party, organized in honor of three young ladies visiting the Greens in August 1893, must have been a sort of competition to determine who could attire himself in the most outlandish manner. One of the guests of honor "decorated herself in a garb of cabbage leaves from head to foot," complete with cabbage leaf fan, whose "delicate perfumes" were "equal to the fumes of a Dutch kitchen just before dinner." Two other guests appeared in black face, one "with that delicate, greasy complection*[sic]* that vasoline*[sic]* and burnt cork . . . only can make." Another's "hair" was made from an unusual combination of materials, among them an Angora goat rug, the mane and tail of a recently dead Shetland pony, and parts of a hair mattress. Thirteen-year-old Jennie dressed up as a Japanese, complete with "the lid of a cloth's*[sic]* hamper to represent the flat straw hat of that country." After dancing, the seventeen bizarrely clad guests took turns entertaining with their respective talents: readings, recitations, songs, and other burlesque-like presentations. Naturally this party warranted several columns on the front page of the local newspaper in an article entitled "Fun at the Falls," whose tone reflects the buffoonery of the occasion itself and whose author numbered among the guests.[4]

In a different type of entertainment, the Green household transformed the front porch of the mansion into a beautiful stage decorated with ferns and Japanese lanterns, which also lined the "avenue" leading to the house. On this occasion the locals, sometimes in costume, presented readings, songs, or dances in an effort to raise money for their church. However Ella, who was supposed to have directed the show, became ill and was unable to attend.[5]

Ella recovered sufficiently, though, to travel by train to the World's Fair in Chicago two months later in September 1893. This journey away from the Falls was one of the Greens' many attempts to find entertainment on the "outside." Probably because her husband was too busy with fall harvest and his other businesses to make the trip, family friend J. Fry Lawrence served as escort and took care of the travel details for Ella and sixteen-year-old Preston. Although the younger siblings remained behind, twenty-three year-old Willis joined his mother and brother en route. On this excursion they viewed the grounds of the Fair from a carriage, attended a baseball game, traveled by rail to visit St. Paul, and from there went to Minneapolis, Minnesota. Along the way they stopped to take a boat ride in the Dells of Wisconsin and in Minneapolis viewed the Falls of Minnehaha. Ella and Preston also saw St. Paul by carriage before returning to Chicago; then both occupied a separate sleeping berth on the return trip to Louisville. This tour, including all their activities, hotel stays, and rail fares, cost Lafayette Green approximately $78.00, including a ten-dollar expense for Preston an overcoat.[6]

When the children were younger, their "outside" entertainments usually consisted of excursions to Frankfort, Louisville, or Rumsey, relatives' hometowns. But Louisville offered the greatest variety of diversions, including "the Exposition," with such attractions as "the fat baby, the Sphinx, and Punch & Judy." Seldom did the entire family leave the Falls simultaneously for such trips, just as they did not for the World's Fair vacation.[7]

The entire Green family, or those not in school, sometimes did travel to Florida together, usually in late winter or early spring. There they spent a few weeks near Fort Reid, basking in the sunshine and enjoying the fresh produce of the area. In 1887, however, Ella did not go to Florida with other family members because she felt well and did not want to risk illness. The next year she made the trip south, but Lafayette and Preston returned to Kentucky without her; she had grown ill with neuralgia and a fever and did not feel up to the journey home. On at least one occasion the family made a visit to Ella's brother, John Orlando Scott, in Sherman, Texas.[8]

From the late 1870s forward, the Greens continued their Florida visits, which by the 1880s and 90s had generally become annual occurrences. However, occasional bouts with sickness continued to interrupt vacation plans as well as everyday life at Falls of Rough. In fact, issues of health were ever present, for in this era of medicine and in a region far

removed from the urban centers that offered the latest in preventions and treatments, poor health could quickly become a
fatality.

Chapter Eight

"Half of the Pleasure of Life is Lost on Being Sick"

Illness—fear of it, worry concerning it, and care for it—engaged many of Ella's thoughts and employed much of her energy. When the health of the community was not a distraction, the family's maladies (including her own) and especially their preventions, treatments, and possible remedies preoccupied her. Perhaps the loss of her first-born at the age of one year had intensified her maternal concern, specifically during periods of epidemics.

In 1875 Falls of Rough inhabitants suffered with persistent coughs, which brought them at all hours of the day and night to the Green home for whiskey. Then the community experienced an epidemic of the "flux" in 1883, when many children grew sick or died, and again in 1884, when "malarial flux" was responsible for two deaths. In that same year raftsmen who traveled to the Falls without knowledge of their exposure to measles received the blame for several additional deaths. In 1887 typhoid fever resulted in numerous fatalities, and two or three years afterwards the area suffered from milk sickness, which also claimed a number of victims. At other times when an epidemic plaguing the Bluegrass Region spared her own community, Ella invited friends and family members to "escape" to the fresh "country air" of the Falls. There, she insisted during an 1873 outbreak of cholera in Louisville, they would not "be tempted with fruit ripe or unripe, [would have] plenty of wholesome diet[,] milk fresh from the cow & . . . [be] clear out of the atmosphere of that terrible disease."[1]

Escape was a common remedy for the Greens when disease threatened. They often retreated to Grayson Springs, where the salubrious sulphur water and change of scenery offered their healing qualities. Lafayette, suffering in 1873 with "billious*[sic]*" attacks, "chills & torpid liver," spent approximately a week at the Springs. At times when travel to such resorts was not an option, the Greens nevertheless sought the sulphur elixir, whether for recuperation from childbearing or stomach disorders or skin irritations.[2]

In some cases family members escaped to a city miles away—usually Frankfort or Louisville—so that Ella and the children could leave behind the place she described as "always damp & moldy," although her husband told her she imagined "half of it." After only two years of marriage, Ella had urged Lafayette to move to a more favorable climate. She probably had in mind Florida, a popular destination for those in Ella's parents' society; Mr. and Mrs. Scott, who both suffered with sundry infirmities, owned a farm there where they fled Kentucky's harsh winters. Mr. and Mrs. Green and family sometimes joined the Scotts at their Silver Lake home, where they believed the sun, warm air, and fresh fruit offered extraordinary healing potential.[3]

The Green family seemed to need respites from sickness, as at least one or two of the family endured some malady at any given time. As a child Willis suffered with "catarrh," a condition his mother believed he had inherited from her father. Ella herself suffered with digestive problems most of her life and complained often of "headache and dyspepsia." Eye problems also plagued her (as they did her father) and caused her at age twenty-nine to wear a blindfold for two weeks. The following year she complained of neuralgia pains enduring four to five hours daily and hurting so badly that it was "worse than twenty teeth aching at the same moment"; twenty-two years later she continued to complain of the same discomfort. Lafayette also reported bouts of neuralgia, with his condition effecting teeth so sore he could hardly chew. Rheumatism in her hands and shoulders also troubled Ella in her early forties and thereafter. When these problems did not seriously interfere with life and epidemics were not a factor, bilious attacks, the chills, or a cold commonly affected some of the family, often canceling their plans or in some other way interrupting their pleasure.[4]

These maladies' treatments, both the ones produced from the doctor's bag as well as those from the cabinet, were often a matter of conjecture. Home treatments, in addition to whiskey and sulphur water, included brandy and morphine, and sometimes a combination of both. Once when Lafayette was "wild with toothache" and had tried "all kinds of local treatment," he admitted he "finally had to resort to morphine and brandy," taking them until he was "entirely insensible" before feeling some relief. And on multiple occasions the local doctor prescribed opiates for the family, including the children, at least once for the "itch" (actually poison oak) and again as a "check" for a disease until its victim could undertake a suitable "course of treatment." In a bout with "skin irruptions" that affected several family members, the doctor prescribed their taking calomel (a compound of mercury and chloride), after which Ella was directed "to rub them . . . with sulphur and lard."[5]

For her own stomach ailment Ella tried several remedies. Her standard treatment was to eat prudently and sparingly, at times finding "that starvation is the only remedy." At other times she drank a tonic obtained from her physician brother in Louisville, or she took a combination of iron and quinine, which she credited with improving a deficient appetite. During one of her more prolonged periods of distress with this problem, an acquaintance of Lafayette shipped her two dozen bottles of Schlitz beer with hopes that it would prove helpful. Unfortunately, the malady persisted. No wonder Ella would declare, after years of suffering and helping to nurse others as well as herself, that "half of the pleasure of life is lost on being sick."[6]

Although Ella probably spoke in general terms concerning illness' effects, she suffered especially keenly from her own illnesses—not only from the pain of the infirmity, but from the cessation of her industry and the resulting boredom. She characterized her family, the Scotts, as being restless and unable to be idle. During the waning months of 1895, Ella's activities became increasingly hindered by her chronic stomach ailments. Most likely the 30th Annual Convention of the Kentucky Sunday School Union, held in Lexington on 13, 14, and 15 August and to which she was a delegate, was Ella's last public outing. In early December she wrote her physician brother that she was "tempted to give up" due to her deteriorating health. She informed him of a recent weight gain of ten pounds but doubted it to be "legitimate flesh, as the abdomen is so large." Reporting that only a standing position offered her any comfort, her letter seems a distressed plea for help.[7]

A 28 February 1896 article in the *Owensboro Daily Messenger* announced the poor state of Ella's health, describing her as "hopelessly ill . . . with cancer and Bright's disease and . . . expected to live but a short time." Twelve days later the same newspaper published notice of her 9 March death: "Mrs. Lafe Green. Death at Last Comes to the Relief of This Estimable Woman." The article attributed her death to stomach cancer. Severe pain and impending death had not prevented her typical efficiency; Ella had already made her funeral arrangements, including her choice of pall bearers. Her body lay first in the Louisville home of her brother Preston, where it remained until it was moved on 11 March to the city of her childhood home for funeral services. Rebecca Eleanor "Ella" Scott Green was buried in the Frankfort Cemetery alongside her parents.[8]

Letters expressing emotions ranging from disbelief to sorrow to optimistic hopes continued to arrive at the Green manor house from immediately before the public announcement of her fatal illness in February until early May. The lament of a nephew, Rumsey Scott, probably represents well the sentiments of many: "She always was so jolly, good natured and kind hearted to everyone. She had always been so lovely and generous to me and I can recall many and many pleasant weeks I have spent with her and the family at the Falls." Illness, which had consumed so much of Ella's joy, had finally claimed her life. Her family and her community mourned their great loss.[9]

View of Falls of Rough, Kentucky, circa 1890 Courtesy Mary O'Neill, Falls of Rough

Chapter Nine

"Only Second to Chicago"

*T*he last half of the nineteenth century in the United States was a time of great change, both technologically and economically. Inventors marketed their timesaving and more energy efficient machines, and investors made and lost great fortunes all in a matter of days. The opportunity to acquire wealth was available to those lucky enough to inherit a good start as well as to those who began with nothing. Whichever the category, dedication and ability were most often the common denominators of success. Lafayette Green inherited a good beginning, but he also possessed great ability and the drive necessary to participate in the economic boom that characterized the times.

Although Lafayette's uncle had carved a small baronage out of the wilderness of western Kentucky during the Commonwealth's infancy, his nephew Lafayette forged that beginning into a business empire. The diversity of his holdings eventually involved Lafayette in farming, grain and lumber milling, retail merchandising, railroad building, gas and oil speculating, and banking; in addition, he practiced law and participated in the politics of his state. Manipulating such varied enterprises required good business sense, hard work, considerable risk taking and, in some cases, luck. Lafayette successfully managed all these components while cultivating both honor and refinement.

From the earliest introduction to his ultimate destiny, Lafayette Green displayed the characteristics necessary for his future success. No indications suggest he ever resisted the responsibility thrust upon him, almost as if he knew from early manhood that he must willingly accept his fate. Even as an eighteen- and nineteen-year-old, whether he was acting as salesman for products of the Falls, apprenticing at Louisville businesses, or studying law, Lafayette apparently accomplished his tasks with a serious sense of duty and responsibility.

Age twenty-six when his uncle died, Lafayette acquired total charge of the extensive affairs that the Falls comprised. The businesses not only continued with little interruption, but the pace of growth soon quickened as well. Lafayette made numerous annual business trips to Louisville, Cincinnati, and as far west as Dubuque, Iowa, trying to find markets for the growing quantity of goods the Falls produced. If anything typified his life during this time, it was long hours and hard work. To acquaint her with his typical day, Lafayette wrote Ella just after their engagement in 1866 that he rose at five each morning, set the field hands to work at six-thirty, checked livestock, took care of business at the store, traveled through the neighborhood buying hogs and tobacco, and did not finish until after supper, when he had to complete correspondence obligations.[1]

On one occasion in 1868, his father-in-law, learning that Lafayette had bought an additional farm, expressed admiration for his industry by stating that Lafayette never "flags or falters." Robert Scott was so impressed with Lafayette's ability that in January 1869 he offered to sell him his own beloved farm at Locust Hill on very generous terms. Scott would sell him the 787-plus acres for $50,000 ($94,500 was the asking price) and advance Ella her one-seventh inheritance of the property, leaving Lafayette to pay only $30,834 over a three-year period. Farming no longer seemed attractive to the aging Mr. Scott and, in addition to chronic health problems, may have played a part in his generous proposal. Lafayette declined the offer, however, deciding to remain at Falls of Rough.[2]

Managing his farm of thousands of acres spread over several counties including Grayson, Breckinridge, and Ohio, plus several hundred acres in Prairie County, Arkansas, was a full-time job for Lafayette. Grayson County tax records for 1886 indicate that the Green properties totaled 3,600 acres in that county alone. Some of Lafayette's more time-consuming

Neighbor children on the Greens' shetland ponies, circa 1898
Courtesy Mary O'Neill, Falls of Rough

responsibilities included planting in the spring, harvesting in the fall, and stripping and prizing tobacco along with hog-killing in the winter; daily chores entailed caring for livestock consisting of horses, mules, cows, sheep, goats and, in this unusual case, Shetland ponies. Lafayette held a particular fondness for these animals that he sold all over the Midwest and for which the farm was famous. These ponies were also favorites of Lafayette's children, particularly his three sons, and also of the neighbor children. The Green boys rode the ponies to school on occasion and exhibited and sold them at county fairs.[3]

Lafayette paid particular attention to his lumber business, which earned him large profits whether in raw timber or milled lumber. Producing crossties for railroad use was particularly lucrative and comprised a large part of Lafayette's

Downriver view of bridge and sawmill, Falls of Rough, circa 1900
Courtesy Mary O'Neill, Falls of Rough

business. He was able to supply a variety of lumber because hardwood forests of ash, oak, hickory, cherry, poplar, and walnut covered the hills surrounding the Falls, the latter wood bringing a premium price. These prime forests remained relatively untapped, even though the site had supported a sawmill since the early 1800s. With numerous streams on or near the property, the logs generally traveled to mills and markets by being rolled into the waterways and then lashed together to await a spring "freshet," which allowed them to float to their destinations.[4]

A favorite pastime at the Falls during these "freshets" was to watch the rafts of logs go over the mill dam; and the number of logs as well as spectators could be enormous. On the first flood of the season in March and April 1888, fifteen thousand logs crossed over the dam, where so many raftsmen and sightseers congregated that eight-year-old Preston wrote to his brother Willis at college proclaiming the "creek is lined with rafts and the men are like blackbirds. They have eat*[sic]* a barrel of crackers and all the caned [canned] fruit and [bought] all the meal and flour to take down the river with them." In April Lafayette indicated 350 to four hundred men were there and that "they eat *[sic]* out everything at the store & bought all the meal & flour in the mill & surrounding country, and many of them went to the Hotel and I expect pretty well eat*[sic]* out Mr. Peyton [the hotel manager]." So the Falls lumber industry, in addition to its own profits, provided the Greens residual benefits.[5]

Lafayette replaced the original sawmill, located near the gristmill on the Grayson County side of Rough River, in 1893 with a more modern one located on the Breckinridge County side. But the original sawmill continued to operate until 1895, when it became a part of the gristmill. Photographs from the times and interviews with local citizens indicate that a water powered tram system pulled the logs into the mills and that the millhands simply threw the refuse slabs

Sawmill on the Breckinridge County side of Rough River, circa 1920
Courtesy Mary O'Neill, Falls of Rough

into the river to be washed away by the next flood.[6]

Even though the power of the river was a necessity to the milling business, it could be a curse as well as a blessing and allowed very little control. If there was no rain for an extended period, the river might not supply enough water to run the turbines, thereby preventing operation of the mills. A flooded river, on the other hand, also interrupted operation of the mills because the turbines would not work properly in high water. Either of these situations cost Lafayette money. As annoying as these problems were, the frequent need to rebuild the dam as a result of flooding proved most bothersome because reconstruction involved considerable effort, time, and expense. Lafayette finally solved this problem when, in 1887 or 1888, he replaced the wooden dam with stone quarried on the property, most likely with stone mason

John Monahan in charge. From this point forward the milling business proceeded with fewer interruptions.[7]

All Lafayette needed to complete the potential of his emerging business empire was a faster and more efficient means of transportation, especially for shipping products to markets. Rivers could no longer effectively supply all the transportation needs of the various enterprises; they needed a railroad. Even though the 1880s saw extensive railroad construction, Falls of Rough, in its isolation, did not figure prominently into the route planning of most railroad companies.

For many years the nearest railroad was the Paducah and Elizabethtown, which passed through Caneyville fifteen miles to the south. By the late 1880s the Louisville, St. Louis and Texas (originally the Louisville, Henderson and Texas) completed construction from West Point (a small town just west of Louisville) to Henderson. Coinciding with this construction was a railroad proposed by Senator R. S. Triplett of Owensboro, called the Owensboro, Falls of Rough and Green River Railroad. This line planned to run from Owensboro through Ohio and Grayson Counties to Leitchfield. Falls of Rough, one of the towns through which the railroad planned to pass, would soon get its much needed railroad—or so many believed.[8]

Railroad excitement in the area reached a fever pitch in 1888. The company obtained right-of-ways, voters approved subscription monies (sometimes nearly unanimously), and surveyors began work; everything seemed to be progressing as planned. Then several landowners, disgruntled over easement settlements, sued the railroad company, delaying building progress. By the time the railroad finally arrived in Fordsville (fifteen miles west) in late September 1889, the company had long since abandoned plans to extend the line through Falls of Rough.

Frustrated with the early delays in construction of the

Owensboro, Falls of Rough and Green River Railroad, Lafayette joined an effort to extend a track from Fordsville to Irvington on the Louisville, St. Louis and Texas Railroad line. This line, chartered 24 February 1888 and called the Louisville, Hardinsburg and Western Railroad, planned to contain a five mile branch from Dempster (approximately ten miles northeast of Fordsville) to Falls of Rough. Excitement about this possibility prompted a friend of Lafayette's son to prophesy the future of the Falls: "The place will be only second to Chicago."[9]

Before the proposed line could become a reality, however, the citizens of Breckinridge County, specifically those in the precincts along the proposed route, needed to vote for a subscription of sixty thousand dollars of stock in the company and furnish the right-of-way. Citizens held debates on the issue throughout the precincts, with Lafayette and several members of his family attending one such debate between Will Hayes, who was against the tax, and a Judge Mercer. The subscription passed in an election held sometime near 10 June 1888. In late 1889 Lafayette, known as "Colonel Lafe," became president of the Louisville, Hardinsburg and Western Railroad Company, and by end of 1890 the company had constructed track from Fordsville to McQuady (eleven miles north of the Falls), including the five-mile branch to Falls of Rough. The once remote community had its railroad! By 6 July 1891 the line was complete to Irvington and thirteen months later became a part of the "Texas" Company, which went into receivership 7 August 1893. It emerged in 1896 as the Louisville, Henderson and St. Louis Railroad, and finally joined the Louisville and Nashville Railroad in 1905.[10]

Life at the Falls no longer reflected the isolation that had characterized it for so many years. Not only could the Greens more easily export their commodities, but now people could more conveniently move back and forth to the outside world. For the first time the external amenities and pleasures

Colonel Lafayette "Lafe" Green, circa 1885
Courtesy Mary O'Neill, Falls of Rough

View of gristmill and sawmill, circa 1885   Courtesy Mary O'Neill, Falls of Rough

were available, like the circus that came to the Falls in 1895. Falls of Rough experienced an increase in visitors, many traveling from the city to enjoy camping, hunting, and fishing, activities they considered part of an idyllic country life. A group of Louisville businessmen headed by J. Fry Lawrence, Lafayette's long-time friend, formed the Kentucky Fish and Game Club, which built a clubhouse at the Falls. On occasion special trains arrived at the Falls carrying just such businessmen as Mr. Lawrence and fellow club members.[11]

The location's reputation as a "getaway" must have spread quickly, for in 1895 Willis wrote to his sister that "many business people have been at the Falls fishing[,] from wealthy men in their private [railroad] cars to "clod-hoppers on foot." He went on to tell her that the hotel was full and "people are wrapped in blankets in the woods sleeping."[12]

In early January 1907 Lafayette and two other investors, C. V. Robertson and J. M. Howard, further diminished the Falls' isolation when they constructed a telephone line to the outside. This new line augmented the closed telephone system that some of the Falls community had enjoyed since 1886.[13]

Lafayette expanded his interests somewhat when he became a major stockholder and president of the Caneyville Natural Gas Company, which claimed capital stock of one million dollars. He also speculated in additional gas ventures and perhaps other natural resources, but none of these investments seem to have contributed substantially to his profits.[14]

In the early 1880s Lafayette revived the political career he had abandoned in the early 1860s. He was elected in 1881 to the Kentucky Senate from the counties of Grayson, Breckinridge, Hancock, and Edmondson. Breckinridge and Grayson Counties' vote totals offer some indication of Lafayette's popularity; he won Breckinridge County by nearly a two-to-one margin over opponent W. H. Parrish and Grayson County by an almost twelve-to-one margin. As a senator Lafayette accepted assignments to the committees of Libraries and Public Buildings and Offices, Banks and Insurance, Federal Relations, and Privileges and Elections. His legislative activities involved the typical duties of sponsoring bills for the benefit of people in his district. Among others, he introduced bills to "improve highways in Breckinridge and Grayson County"; "amend the charter of the town of Cloverport"; and to "prohibit the sale of spiritous, vinous, or malt liquors in the Spring Lick and Caneyville precincts of Grayson County." At the end of his term in 1884, Lafayette chose not to seek reelection and to end his political career.[15]

Lafayette's businesses, operating as L. Green and Son, continued to grow, expand, and profit as the new century drew near. Though approaching age sixty-five, he continued to be actively engaged in his businesses and also enjoyed the benefit of his sons as partners. In addition, he continued to travel to Florida occasionally for social and health benefits, although his health was not a consummate concern. However, just as he planned to meet his daughter, who was visiting friends in Atlanta, within a few days for a trip to Naples, Florida, where the family sometimes wintered, the unforeseen occurred. While sitting in the library of his house just past noon on 28 January 1907, Lafayette "complained of sharp pains in the chest and remarked that he thought that they came from a spell of indigestion." He apparently had just eaten dinner and gone into the library to rest for a few minutes before returning to work, his three sons nearby. Shortly thereafter he collapsed and the physician summoned recorded the cause of death as "heart failure."[16]

Telegrams arrived from all across the Commonwealth as well as from other states, presenting evidence of the distinction Lafayette had obtained through his political and business careers. One long-time friend, transplanted Kentuckian and former Missouri governor, Thomas T. Crittenden, upon hearing of Lafayette's death, appended his letter of condolence with words of praise: "The earth that bears the dead, Bears not alive a nobler gentleman." Lafayette Green was buried beside his wife in the Frankfort Cemetery, Frankfort, Kentucky. A second generation had ended.[17]

Even though Falls of Rough obviously did not become a "second Chicago," it did rate a modest entry in the *Kentucky Gazatteer and Business Directory 1895-1896*. The entry listed a population of 250, a post office, Western Union telegraph office, train station, general store, gristmill, and sawmill. It further recorded the town as having a Methodist minister, Rev. W. W. Lambreth; blacksmith, Lewis Richards; stonemason, John Monahan; postmaster, Lafayette Green; physician, Robert T. Demster; railroad express agent, Samuel Morgan; hotel manager, F. W. Peyton; and coal miner, S. Allen.[18]

As such, Falls of Rough prepared to begin its third generation, with the children of Ella and Lafayette Green its new stewards. But before they could assume their roles, the younger Greens required a proper foundation. Their ambitious parents dutifully advocated and supervised the preparations necessary to help insure the success of their posterity.

Chapter Ten

"Fail Is a Word We Know Nothing About"

Almost from birth, each of the four children of Lafayette and Eleanor Green was admonished to excel. Excellence in this case implied "live up to the wonderful examples set by your ancestors," particularly members of the Scott and related families. On occasion their mother provided specific ancestors as examples, such as Reverends William and Robert Breckinridge; but most often she invoked the name of her father, Robert Wilmot Scott. Ella, along with her brothers and sisters, adored her father, a man with extensive knowledge, fine moral character, few vices, and a strong aversion to the use of alcohol. Ella hoped her children would emulate their grandfather and frequently reminded them of his exemplary behavior; she also offered their father as a role model.[1]

Of the four children Willis, the oldest, felt the weight of his ancestors' legacy most acutely. In the mind of his mother, Willis was the one to set the example by excelling in his school work and, particularly, in his moral character. To help ensure the accomplishment of both these goals, Ella insisted

102

that thirteen-year-old Willis enroll in the Kentucky Military Institute, located in the small community of Farmdale, six miles south of Frankfort and near her beloved Locust Hill. The strict discipline of military training for which KMI was reputed would afford the young man excellent guidance for building an honorable future as well as superior preparation for college.[2]

While at the Institute, young Willis excelled in his academic work. His first quarter grade report lists all grades in the "excellent" category except spelling; so outstanding was his work during the first weeks that the Institute's superintendent, Robert Allen, indicated Willis as the best in his class. Willis wrote his grandfather Scott in 1884, "I stand among the front rank in my classes," suggesting his awareness of his relatives' standards and expectations, especially those of his grandfather. But Willis was not dedicated exclusively to the studious life while in Farmdale. Because his father was in the Kentucky Senate in nearby Frankfort, on occasion they enjoyed each other's company at special events. Willis also found pleasure in his sojourns into Frankfort, visits with relatives who lived in the area, and occasional weekends in their homes. Meanwhile, he remained conscientious, maintained his high grade standards, and graduated the Institute in June 1885.[3]

After his KMI graduation the fifteen-year-old prepared to enter the next stage of his education. Willis entertained ideas of going to Harvard to become a lawyer like his father but, instead, in the fall of 1885 entered Centre College at Danville. This Presbyterian college was, as it remains today, renowned for its academic excellence and famous alumni, who include two of Willis' maternal uncles. Another of his relatives, Rev. William L. Breckinridge, was a past president of the college. This precedent suggests that Willis' enrollment in Centre was probably a family decision rather than his own. So with ancestors watching and a mother insisting upon excellence by admonishing that "fail is a word we know nothing about," Willis entered college life. His mother's admonishments and advice about the future continued throughout his academic career, with her letters including such encouragements as "Upward & onward, my boy—must be your motto—& no fail" and "make something more of yourself than a merchant." He had expectations to meet![4]

Willis apparently had no difficulty adapting to campus life at Centre. In a letter to his mother in November of his sophomore year, he remarked, "The college influence has been such that I feel that I am drifting steadily towards the Presbyterian and the first thing I know I will be a Republican." During his four years at Centre, Willis maintained a superior academic record while also indulging in the social functions of college life, particularly the Greek fraternities. He was responsible during his second year there for inaugurating a chapter of Sigma Alpha Epsilon; approximately six months later he had resigned from this fraternity and was acting as secretary to the Alpha Chapter of Phi Delta Theta. Apparently Willis' enterprising solicitation of former fraternity members for contributions was responsible for the latter fraternity's obtaining its own hall.[5]

Although he was exemplary in most aspects of college life, Willis probably preferred that some of his deeds be kept from his mother, whose constant admonishments against the evils of alcohol apparently went unheeded. If letters from friends provide an accurate indication, Willis failed drastically to live up to the temperance legacy of his grandfather, for several items of correspondence contain recollections of bibulous social occasions.[6]

Letters from friends also testify to Willis' considerable interest in the opposite sex. While his parents would have endorsed such interest, they would not have approved some of his correspondents' comments about the young women he knew; references tend toward the risque and, in some cases, quite near vulgarity. Such accounts could have simply been bravado from one young man to another. But even though such impropriety existed among his male friends, more instances of gentlemanly behavior, such as sending flowers to special girls, reflected the efforts and expectations of his upbringing. The latter behavior must have prevailed, for Willis continued to command attention of the young ladies in the "proper" social circles and constantly received invitations from them to serve as their escort to social affairs. Although few letters suggest Willis' involvement in a serious relationship, one does reveal an anxiety that might have contributed to his failure to ever marry. A male correspondent, who addressed twenty-year-old Willis as "Dear Old Lady," encouraged him to marry the girl with whom he was so "much in love," adding, "Put away your foolish fear of a henpecked life, and get married at once."[7]

Ella was not only demanding as a mother but also extremely protective, regularly sending Willis packages of food and instructing him to take care of his health, particularly his eyes. At about the age of eleven, Willis had sustained an injury to an eye and wore an artificial one the rest of his life. His own references to the limitation of his eyesight are essentially nonexistent, but at least one episode involving the false eye suggests Willis apparently never considered it more than a minor inconvenience. In a letter to his grandfather Scott, he related that while visiting his aunt in Frankfort he had left the eye at bedtime on a bedside table; when he awoke the next morning, it was missing. After searching the entire house, he concluded that because rats were plentiful in the house, one of the rodents must have carried off his eye. In addition to concern about his eyesight, his mother's protectiveness included regular warnings against exposing himself to inclement weather, contagious diseases, and undesirable companions.[8]

Less demanding than his wife, Lafayette was apparently an attentive and quite indulgent parent. During his years at

Centre, Willis regularly received letters from his father, often with generous checks enclosed. Ella may have thought at times that Lafayette was too indulgent, for she advised Willis on occasion not to take advantage of his father's generosity.[9]

As a student at Centre, Willis showed a special interest in oratory and was a member of Centre's oratorical society. As a member of this group he competed in several contests and gave a speech entitled "The Civilizations of the Ages" at the 1888 school commencement. If the professor's evaluation of the speech was a true appraisal, its success was less than spectacular. Willis again delivered a speech, this one entitled "Mental Development," at his own commencement in 1889. Evaluation cards completed by fellow students and then returned to the speaker suggest this speech was an improvement over the one of the previous year.[10]

Willis' 1889 graduating class numbered only eight but included a future governor of Kentucky, Augustus O. Stanley. And although Willis graduated with an excellent academic standing, he had not satisfied his mother's aspirations for him. She expressed gratitude that Willis had graduated in the top of his class, but commented, "My over running ambition was not satisfied, want to see your name above all others." Willis' aspirations to obtain a Harvard law degree yielded to his father's need for help in running his numerous businesses, and soon after his Centre graduation Willis went to work at the Falls, never to realize the hoped-for law degree.[11]

The Greens' second son, Preston, seven years younger than Willis, was not made to feel quite the same pressure for satisfying ancestral expectations. During 1894 he and cousin Sam Major, Jr., the son of Ella's oldest sister Mary, attended boarding school in Hardinsburg. Sam was the same age as Preston and had come to live with the Greens upon being orphaned at the age of nine. After extending his boarding school education somewhat, eighteen-year-old Preston followed his older brother's example and in 1895 entered Centre College as a sophomore; his cousin Sam entered the Naval Academy at Annapolis.[12]

Unfortunately, only a small amount of correspondence remains between Preston and his immediate family. Perhaps Preston was a reluctant correspondent. Or, although no such proof exists, the lack of his correspondence might have been the result of an alleged quarrel that developed between Preston and his sister Jennie, the last of the siblings to survive and, consequently, the one in charge of preserving or destroying family papers. While the cause of this long-standing disagreement is a matter of much speculation, perhaps it simply resulted from Preston's wry sense of humor, which may have "worn thin" with his more serious sister.

Preston's inability to pass up an opportunity for witticism, or even a prank, shows in a letter he wrote while at Centre to his family. The letter's style and tone offers remarkable insight into the young Preston's wit and comportment, and its contents also reveal something of the atmosphere of Centre College in the late 1890s. This 19 February 1896 letter, which contains numerous mistakes in grammar and mechanics, has the salutation "Dear M.P.W.J.R." (Mama, Papa, Willis, Jennie, Robert), and is written largely in dialogue. Preston first chided members of the family, particularly his sixteen-year-old sister Jennie, for not writing to him, saying it should be "a pleasant relief for her from sitting up & holding her hands to drop me a short letter of some 20 pages or so." His letter continues:

> Tell Willis Prof. Jackie was enquiring about him today. "What's that brother of yours doing now Green dont any body come to the store this kind of weather do they? Settin by the fire and smoking his pipe I guess." I told him you didnt stay in

the store now but was running the sawmill.
"Dont mind out he'll get his head sawed off fool-
ing around a saw mill." He'll be a sawed off man
then wont he Professor? He started at me with a
ruler in his hand and I went out the door like I
was shot out of a gun. We are in Botany now
now *[sic]* and about a week ago he said to me:
"Do all flowers bloom Green? and like a sucker I
said yes Sir. Dont any thing of the kind some of
them bloom red and all sorts of colors: Now just
look a there, there was that fellows brother that
went to school here to me and there wasn't a
smarter fellow in the whole class and just look at
him (referring to me) hasn't got any more sense
than to set up there and tell me all plants bloom
green. But I got him good the other day.

      Somebody was talking about what
a long ear of corn they had seen somewhere and
he pretended like he didnt hear them say ear of
and jumped up and said who ever heard of a corn
and of course the whole class commenced to
laugh just to please him when they had about
quieted down I hopped up and said I have Prof, I
got one on my foot now. Everybody just
hollered. I would have given five dollars afterwards if I hadn't said it for I ll [I'll] bet he'll make
[me] sorry of it but it was just too good to keep.
I must close now to get this letter off and I have
my doubts as to its getting off now.

      With love to all, I remain
      Son, Brother & Co.[13]

If Preston's demeanor was such toward his professors, one can only imagine the many pranks and jokes he initiated at his baby sister's expense.

Grade records indicate that Preston was a rather inferior student, failing or nearly failing several subjects. And other than being a member of the Chamberlain Philosophical and Literary Society, he apparently was not active in any other campus organizations. He completed his junior year but did not return the next year; his failure to do so was probably a result of his poor class standing and his lack of interest.[14]

Although Jennie, sometimes called Jean or Jeannie by family members, was Lafayette and Ella's only surviving daughter, she did not have the same expectations placed upon her as did her brothers. While she would not enter Centre College nor necessarily need to measure up to her ancestors' performances, nevertheless, she would assuredly have to meet her parents'—and particularly a father's—expectations. They gave her the best opportunities available to a young lady of the time. As she approached the age when her education required more than that offered by home school, Lafayette searched for a proper institution for her. His considerations included The Western, a college and seminary for women in Oxford, Ohio, but Jennie ultimately enrolled in the Princeton Collegiate Institute in Princeton, Kentucky.[15]

Jennie entered the Institute in September 1894 and completed one full scholastic year. Probably due to her excellent home schooling, the school classified her as a sophomore for all her classes except Latin, in which she received promotion to a junior. The rest of her schedule included rhetoric, algebra, history, French, physics, drawing, music, and Bible. This schedule proved so demanding, at least according to Jennie, that she asked her parents' permission to drop physics. Jennie, perhaps facetiously, indicated in a letter that October that her parents would not recognize her because she had grown thin and pale from "hard studying." However, she did

Jennie Green, circa 1896
Courtesy Mary O'Neill, Falls of Rough

seem genuinely concerned about her "marks," for she occasionally requested her parents to forward her monthly reports so that she, too, could know her progress.[16]

Both Ella and Lafayette showed great concern for their daughter's welfare and were especially attentive on her behalf. Jennie regularly received packages from home containing everything from "eatables" to clothes. Once she received a new winter coat and shoes—both unrequested and entirely a surprise—and, on another occasion, a desk specifically from her father. At a different time, upon hearing that Jennie had a cold, Ella voiced concern that Mr. Richmond, president of the Institute, was not having fires built in the morning for the girls, something "he should have attended to long ago, this is the first boarding school for young ladies where they had to build their own fires." She added, "I think this is the reason why your papa has been in no hurry to pay the bills." Later, when Ella heard that smallpox might be in the Princeton area, she instructed Jennie to be sure to get a vaccination.[17]

Jennie's oldest brother Willis, nine years her senior, was also concerned with his sister's well-being; he even seemed to have a special fondness for her. He corresponded with her often, routinely enclosing a check and urging her to "spend it as you please for the little pleasures" or for "trifles light as air."[18]

Though Jennie suffered with bouts of homesickness in her first few weeks at the Institute, a lack of social activity was not the cause, for she easily became a part of Princeton's social world. Mary Green Lawrence, a music teacher at the school who identified herself as Ella's cousin, wrote that Jennie was "more in demand than any other girl here." She added that Jennie had become a companion to Mary Ratliff, a daughter of one of the leading families in town, whom she described as "a very exclusive haughty & wealthy young miss of fifteen summers." Miss Lawrence had encouraged their relationship, though, because she found Miss Ratliff to also be "an elegant young girl."[19]

Initially Jennie gave indications that she was not interested in boys, prompting her friend Mary Lawrence to comment that Jennie was very indifferent to the opposite sex— more so than any other girl there; but this apparent indifference did not endure. By November a budding love affair was developing between Jennie and Shell Smith, a fellow student at the Institute and the son of an old Princeton family. Letters and notes passed between them at school document this affair, which continued over the next four years even though Jennie was not continuously enrolled at the Institute. Their correspondence, in which he referred to her as "My darling little girl" or simply "Jinks," contains the typical youthful flirtations: inquiries into the other's affection, allusions to secret encounters, anguishes of unresolved love, and closings of "S. W. A. K." (sealed with a kiss). But the youthful love affair faded and transformed into a lifelong friendship, as letters they exchanged in 1933 affirm.[20]

Jennie did not return to the Institute in the fall of 1895, probably due to the worsening condition of her seriously ill mother, who died in March 1896. Jennie spent parts of the following year and a half either at Falls of Rough or in Louisville, perhaps attending boarding school, but she returned to Princeton in the spring of 1897, hoping especially to resume her music studies. However, she remained for only one semester and then returned to the Falls to begin in earnest to run the household.[21]

Robert, three years younger than Jennie and "baby" of the Green family, was typically somewhat spoiled as a child. Family members and acquaintances seemed to be aware of that fact, for one of them wrote Ella to inquire of the family's activities and well-being with suppositions concerning the children's whereabouts. The correspondent accounted for each child except thirteen-year-old Robert, who she presumed surely was not "very far from his mother's wing."[22]

At that time Robert had broken away from his mother somewhat and was attending boarding school in Hardinsburg, where he spent two years. Then in 1898, at age sixteen, he, too, entered Centre College, where he proved to be less than a model student. Jennie, now acting as surrogate mother, reprimanded Robert for the bad spelling in his correspondence. (Ironically, her own letters contained several misspelled words.) She warned, "Papa was so much disgusted and angry with your letter today. Half the words are spelled wrong. He may not let you go back to college unless you do better." Other than the weakness in spelling and a failure in physics his junior year, Robert's grades were average. He was, as Willis had been, a member of the Phi Delta Theta fraternity and, also like his sibling, apparently experienced no problems fitting into college life. No indicators explain why he failed to return to college in the fall of 1901, his senior year, to complete his degree.[23]

Although the children of Lafayette and Eleanor Green did not always live up to their mother and father's lofty expectations, either academically or morally, they nevertheless became well-adjusted, successful adults. The caring attitude and moral integrity of their parents and grandparents, which nourished that success, was evident in many aspects of their adult lives—from their continued concern for their community and mankind in general to their active, though temperate, lifestyles.

The four siblings also emulated their parents' industry and equaled their success, but though four partners divided the tasks previously managed by two, the growth of the Falls did not progress as it had during the previous two generations. However, the fault did not lie in a lack of dedication to their duty. The times were changing—and those changes made all the difference.

Some of the Shetland ponies raised by the Greens
Courtesy Mary O'Neill, Falls of Rough

Robert Green
Courtesy Mary O'Neill, Falls of Rough

*Falls of Rough,
circa 1910
Courtesy
Mary O'Neill,
Falls of Rough*

*Jennie Scott Green (center), circa 1910
Courtesy Mary O'Neill, Falls of Rough*

Preston Scott Green, circa 1878
Courtesy Mary O'Neill,
Falls of Rough

Jennie Scott Green, circa 1920
Courtesy Mary O'Neill,
Falls of Rough

A typical tenant house, circa 1930
Courtesy Louise Q. Hodges, Leitchfield, Kentucky

Mule teams plowing field in front of Green home, circa 1920
Courtesy Louise Q. Hodges, Leitchfield, Kentucky

Effects of tornado around Green mansion, circa 1916
Courtesy Louise Q. Hodges, Leitchfield, Kentucky

"Main Street," Falls of Rough, circa 1940
Courtesy Mary O'Neill, Falls of Rough, Kentucky

Arthur Surrell,
longtime employee
of the Greens
Courtesy
Green Farms Papers,
University of Louisville

Behind Green mansion, 1892 L-R: Jack, Green employee; unidentified man;
Marshall Morris; Lois Morris; S.I.M. Major (age 15); Rumsey W. Scott;
standing Robert Green
Courtesy James and Marion Ferguson, Richmond, Kentucky

Chapter Eleven

"Very Gracious Southern Living"

With the beginning of the new century and the death of Lafayette Green, the last generation of Greens—Willis, Preston, Jennie, and Robert—began their turn as proprietors of the family businesses. And they devoted most of their lives to exactly that. They socialized occasionally, but primarily with those outside Falls of Rough; in addition, their large manor house and affluent status set them farther apart from those who lived around them. To most of the community, they remained an enigma. They were not one entity, obviously, but four distinct individuals who each contributed to the character of the estate and village that progressed into the second half of the twentieth century—and toward its fatal destiny.

The siblings divided the responsibilities for managing the large and varied operations based generally upon individual interests and abilities. Their personalities, temperaments, and styles also cast their influence upon the manner in which they fulfilled those obligations and the subsequent perception of the Falls and its masters.

Kind and soft spoken but frank, Willis, the oldest, exhibited a reserved temperament and easygoing manner, but he seldom smiled. His immaculate attire—dress shirt, tie, spats, and a suitcoat shed only in the height of a Kentucky summer—reflected his serious demeanor. And his habit of placing each hand in a back trouser pocket effected the distinctive carriage of his 5' 10" frame. But those who knew him best remember most his keen mind. Local historian and resident of Falls of Rough, Burl St. Clair described Willis as having an intellect capable even of "running General Motors."[1]

Soon after graduating Centre College in 1889, Willis began to assume more of the business duties at the Falls, for which he demonstrated great acumen. He initially managed the general store, only one of the businesses operating at the time under the name "L. Green and Son," an indication of his new position as partner to his father. By the mid-1890s he had moved to the sawmill and, by the early 1900s, to financial manager of all the enterprises: store, sawmill, gristmill, and farm operations; that management also included investment of the firm's profits in stocks and bonds.

Willis apparently originated the idea of establishing a local bank, incorporated on 21 April 1906 with the title Rough River Bank. The bank began business on 2 June with sixteen original stockholders, who elected Willis president and E. S. Robinson vice president, and a total capital stock of fifteen thousand dollars. The largest stockholders were W. R. Cummings with 30 shares; Willis Green, 29 shares; John J. McHenry, 20 shares; and Lafayette Green, 20 shares, with each share valued at one hundred dollars. Preston Green joined the bank management in 1907 as a member of the Board of Directors, and in 1909 Ferd Frentress became vice president. Willis retained the presidency until the bank's unexplained closing in August 1911. Suggesting a profitable operating status, the minutes of the 4 June 1910 yearly Board of Directors meeting indicate the Board had declared a divi-

Willis Green, circa 1930
Courtesy Mary O'Neill, Falls of Rough

Near the Green flower garden, Robert Green, unidentified couple, Willis Green,
circa 1935
Courtesy Mary O'Neill, Falls of Rough

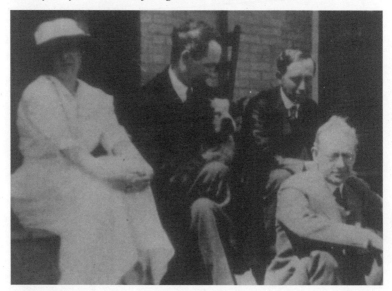

Jennie Green, Willis Green, Robert Green, unidentified man, circa 1910
Courtesy Mary O'Neill, Falls of Rough

dend of nine hundred dollars and raised the cashier's salary from $60 to $62.50 per month.[2]

Willis' position as bank president helped reinforce his prestige among his contemporaries, who remember him as the brother most visible in the general store, where he had an office, and as the one supremely in charge of all operations. A true professional, Willis was adamant that the financial records of which he was in charge be maintained meticulously. He required the bookkeeper to keep four record books, one for each of the four businesses.[3]

When Lafayette died in 1907, the businesses at the Falls began operating under the name of Green Brothers. Preston and Robert began at this point to share more of the responsibilities with Willis.

Preston assumed the duties of running the sawmill and gristmill soon after he left college in 1898. He possessed

Preston Green with young people on bridge, circa 1940
Courtesy Louise Q. Hodges, Leitchfield, Kentucky

an impulsive temperament and was prone on occasion to lose his temper and behave rashly, then just as quickly to dismiss the causal incident. This impulsive behavior prompted some observers who did not know him well to describe him as mean; it was also the reason, according to local stories, he lost a hand while showing a worker how to more quickly and efficiently feed a corn shredder. As a result of his accident, he wore an artificial hand covered by a glove the rest of his life. Those who knew him well considered Preston, outgoing and possessing a keen sense of humor, to be jovial and entertaining, often amusing children in the general store with a sleight of hand trick, after which he awarded them the employed coin.[4]

Unlike his older brother, Preston's style of attire was relaxed, as he most often wore a set of work clothes and seldom donned a coat and tie. Though a hole here and there did not appear to bother him, according to long-time cook and housekeeper Gwyn Spaulding, he requested a clean set of clothing each morning.[5]

Mildred Burton Ridenour, a child growing up a few miles from Falls of Rough in the mid-twenties, recalls "Mr. Preston" as one who enjoyed children, teasing them and offering rides in his car, one of the first in the area. He traveled by her home on one of his "drummer" routes as he solicited orders for or delivered their "Grayson Lily" flour or other products. With a more extroverted, fun-loving, and carefree nature than his brothers, he fit well the public-related tasks required in their milling businesses.

Robert, the youngest sibling, left Centre in 1901 to return home and oversee the extensive farm operations. His fondness for horses suited him for the job, as a large part of his responsibility included riding over the fields each workday to supervise his laborers. He spent most of his day riding his horse or, later, in his car from field to field over a farm so vast that in 1931 the Farm Bureau classified its eight thousand acres as the largest farm in Kentucky. This somewhat solitary

assignment accommodated Robert's quiet and introverted personality. Extremely small in stature, he, like Willis, was kind,
seldom smiled, and also exhibited a serious demeanor. And
like his brother Preston, he seemed unconcerned about his
appearance, preferring work clothes much like those of his
hired hands. Acquaintances recall that he suffered from a
chronic skin condition which effected a habitual scratching of
his arms.[6]

    Jennie, the only sister, was mistress of the house, a role
she inherited at age sixteen upon the death of her mother in
1896. Although she left the Falls for brief periods after that
date, she undertook the full-time responsibility after her
father's death in 1907. Those responsibilities were many,
although a cook, maids, a gardener, and a handyman performed much of the physical labor. During at least the last
twenty or thirty years of her life, Jennie wrote out a menu each
day, probably a habit she had established early in her manage-

*Robert Green
with one of his
favorite horses,
circa 1928
Courtesy
Mary O'Neill,
Falls of Rough*

ment of domestic duties. Her collection of recipes, both those written in her own (almost illegible) hand as well as the large numbers clipped from newspapers and magazines, testifies to her interest in the reputation of her kitchen. According to cook Gwyn Spaulding, by the late 1920s Jennie had experienced difficulty keeping cooks, due mainly to her strict demands and the hard task of "getting along" with her.[7]

Coexisting with the aging Jennie could be a difficult task, although different acquaintances offer disparate portraits of her. One characterized her as a most gracious hostess while another described her as ill tempered and discourteous. Most did agree that she was demanding, headstrong, high tempered, and opinionated. She was also extremely racist, though such an attitude was not uncommon for a Southerner of her era. In 1961 she informed Louisville's Stewart's Dry Goods Company, where she had shopped extensively for sixty years, that she would no longer be a patron if the company was

Jennie Green,
circa 1906
Courtesy James and
Marion Ferguson,
Richmond, Kentucky

127

Watermelon party (Jennie on right)   Courtesy Burl St. Clair, Falls of Rough

"integrating your store to the Negroes." On the other hand, she often sent flowers from her extensive, formal flower garden to friends and family as tokens of her thoughtfulness. Perhaps her severe attitude and actions were only those of an elderly woman and did not typify the young Jennie, who hosted parties for friends, one a five-day excursion for five guests to Mammoth Cave near Bowling Green, Kentucky.[8]

Observers both inside and outside the community recognized Jennie's fondness for—if not preoccupation with—the color green. Her clothes, purchased at some of the most elite stores in Louisville and other cities on her travel itineraries, were almost exclusively green, as was her last car, a 1951 Packard Ultramatic. In addition, much of her household decor and china as well as linens and kitchen utensils sustained her color theme. She even sacrificed a perfectly functioning telephone to her obsession. When a telephone company technician visited the manor house to perform routine phone work in the 1950s, Jennie somehow learned that his truck held a green telephone and insisted that he install it immediately.[9]

Jennie also exhibited an interest in the occult. During at least the last few decades of her life "Miss Jennie" made annual trips to the Chautauqua area of New York, where she sometimes attended sessions of "The World Universal Religion of Spiritualism." A 1954 brochure, which shows obvious signs of use, espouses Lily Dale, New York, site of the annual convention, as "The World Center of Spiritualism." One of the religion's principles defined death as only a "change"; another affirmed "that communication with the so-called dead is a fact, scientifically proven by the phenomena of Spiritualism." Among the three or four daily sessions was generally one or two labeled "Auditorium Seance" and another, "Spirit Greetings."[10]

Jennie frequently employed a Ouija board to communicate with dead relatives and loved ones, particularly her mother and, later, Robert, to whom she had been especially close. According to Agnes Beard, longtime bookkeeper for the Greens, Jennie habitually transcribed these messages from the spirits, which included former beaux, a Dr. Lex from Hardinsburg, in particular. In one "message" from Robert's spirit, written four weeks after his February 1943 death, Jennie seeks reassurance that she had sufficiently cared for her brother in his last days ("Did you feel we deserted you when we left at night?") and guidance for her life without him (Robert "tells" her to look after Willis, who will not admit he needs her, and not to "think of Pres [Preston] with hatred—it makes him sick and hurts your soul."). Robert's "spirit" requests repeatedly, "Don't call me this way" and "Let me alone," as he does not want to be reminded of a "plain" where he was so sick and unhappy. When Jennie inquires about "papa & mama," Robert responds that "they are busy with soldiers." This three-page "message," perhaps the only one to survive Jennie's order that all such notes be destroyed upon her death, displays evidence of having been impulsively recorded, with a lack of concern for grammatical correctness or legibili-ty.[11]

Mrs. Beard related that Jennie frequently sought advice from Robert's "spirit" when Jennie disagreed with a decision Preston had made. She sent Robert's transcribed sug-gestions, usually the same as her own but essentially illegible because she often wrote them with her left hand, via Mrs. Beard to Preston, the brother with whom she had not spoken for years. In addition, Jennie consulted astrological forecasts, such as "A Brief Guide Covering Business, Financial[,] Vocation, Health[,] and Love Affairs, Etc.," a ten-page book-let containing a "scientific astrological analysis for Libra" for 1934 and 1935.[12]

Jennie's position as "general" of the household was the only authority she possessed on her family's estate after September 1911, when she requested her share of the inheri-tance and relinquished any further claims in it to her three brothers. The deed of conveyance indicates she received "one dollar and other valuable consideration" for her one-fourth share. What "valuable consideration" denoted remains a mys-tery as well as does the reason Jennie made such an extreme decision, particularly at the age of thirty-two.[13]

Perhaps an escalating quarrel with Preston caused Jennie's action, although this theory is only speculation. And here, too, exists additional intrigue—what had really precipi-tated such a rift between brother and sister that they did not speak to each other for the last decades of their lives? Two unsubstantiated tales, circulated in the community for years, attempt to explain a cause for the estrangement. One recounts that Jennie found Preston and his girlfriend, a book-keeper who occupied a room in the manor house, in Preston's bedroom and subsequently threw all her belongings out an upstairs window. A second explanation reports that Preston went inside the house immediately after severing his hand and bled onto furnishings and carpet, extensively soiling the house. No one seems to know when the ultimate break between them occurred, and no surviving correspondence documents it.

However, that Preston and Jennie clashed was evident. Jennie acknowledged their long-term disagreement when she told cook Gwyn Spaulding that the two of them had fought

Robert Green (left) and unidentified man escorting Jennie Green to the railroad depot at Falls of Rough, circa 1911
Courtesy Burl St. Clair, Falls of Rough

even as children. Substantiation of that claim appears in a letter their mother wrote between 1885 and 1889, when Jennie was between six and ten years old and Preston eight and twelve. In that letter to Willis, in college at Danville, their mother reported "Jean [Jennie] and Preston are fighting like cats and dogs."[14]

But a cause other than—or in addition to—her dispute with her brother could have prompted Jennie's drastic 1911 decision. She might have simply agreed to her brothers' determination to simplify the legal aspects of the businesses. Men of her era did not consider women as equals, especially in the business world; furthermore, Jennie had no background in their operations. Whatever the reason, almost immediately after giving up her inheritance she embarked upon a trip to Europe, where she spent approximately one year. Afterward she returned to the Falls and continued to run the household, but she never participated in any of the businesses until the last of her brothers died in 1945.

The brother and sister feud probably made all four of the Greens' lives more difficult; after all, not only did they live together in the manor house, but the three brothers also had to work together constantly in their businesses. Robert, who seemed to love Jennie as a mother figure, and Willis, who had

Jennie Green (in white) and a friend waiting for a train at the Falls of Rough depot, circa 1911 Courtesy Burl St. Clair, Falls of Rough

always felt a special fondness for his only sister, needed Preston's cooperation for the success of Green Brothers. There exists no indication that the brothers allowed the quarrel to interfere with their work. It might, however, have contributed somewhat to the manner in which they engaged in leisure and social activities. Each sibling had his own friends and associates; as a result, most of their leisure activities were not family affairs but individualized ones, with each following his or her own interests. On occasion, though, Willis and Jennie vacationed together. In 1933 they toured the northeastern United States, and they often traveled together to Naples, Florida, where they spent part of each winter.[15]

Jennie enjoyed travel and made her first trip to Europe in 1909, when she visited the major European cities, and then a second in 1911 immediately following the surrender of her portion of the inheritance. That second trip became a memorable one. In 1953, when the movie industry released its version of the sinking of the great luxury liner *Titanic*, Jennie related in an interview just how close she had come to the fate of that ship's passengers. She recalled that while returning from Europe in April 1912 on a smaller ship scheduled to dock only hours before the larger liner, "They got us all up at dawn to see that big iceberg. It was clear then and we could see it clearly. Then the fog closed in. That night was a horrible night. Two musicians aboard played all night to keep our courage up." Upon their arrival in New York, the passengers on her ship received news of the *Titanic's* sinking. Jennie further commented, "I've always felt our ship might have had the same fate if we hadn't had a good captain and a slow boat."[16]

Jennie also made several trips to Mexico and often spent a few weeks during the summer in Chautauqua, New York, or Wequetonsing, Michigan. She more frequently traveled by train or later in her chauffeured car to Louisville, always staying in the Brown Hotel, to shop and enjoy the opera and ballet. Her scrapbooks contain numerous clippings from the *Louisville Courier-Journal* of opera and ballet stars.

When she remained at home, the elder Jennie helped fill her leisure time by working in her bi-level flower garden, enclosed in a decorative brick wall and complete with stepping stones and ornamental iron work.[17]

Like Jennie, Willis also was a world traveler. In 1923 he embarked on a trip to the Far East with Japan and China as his primary destinations. Traveling with several members in his entourage, probably friends and relatives, Willis found the trip an unforgettable one—and not only from his experience with the distinct Japanese and Chinese cultures. During their stay in Japan, one of the most devastating earthquakes in the country's history hit the area around Tokyo and Yokohama. Willis wrote relatives in Rumsey, Kentucky, that his train swayed so much from the aftershocks that it almost made him seasick. In 1929 Willis also traveled to Eastern Canada and from there to Europe, where he visited London and Paris.[18]

Preston, less inclined to world travel, instead journeyed each winter to Brighton, Alabama. While he seldom hunted at home, he was an avid bird hunter and generally kept a large number of bird dogs that he transported to Alabama for his hunting vacations.[19]

Although Robert periodically made short trips, including one to Colorado with Willis, he appears to have been the "homebody" of the family. Little indication exists that he enjoyed travel, at least to the extent of his brothers and sister. He was often the only one of his siblings who remained at the Falls during times of vacation to oversee the continuing operations.[20]

While extensive travel engaged much of their time, the routine work necessary to keep the many enterprises at the Falls functioning properly characterized most of the Greens' schedules. Although they did employ foremen and overseerers, particularly the Eskridge brothers—Arlie, Morgan, and Palmer—beginning in the 1910s, the extensive enterprises still required the owners' full-time involvement.

Robert, in charge of the farms, was the early riser, usually at 6:00 A. M. so that he could set the hired help to work in the fields before breakfast at seven. Then promptly at noon, the Greens, following the custom of most southern farms, took their main meal, dinner; supper followed at exactly 6:00 P. M. With the exception of breakfast, the siblings ate in the main dining room, usually in a very proper manner with china and a full set of silverware. In the evening the family members "dressed" for dinner and, if guests were present, formal attire, including long dresses for the ladies, was not uncommon.[21]

Business acquaintance and social companion Martha Brown characterized the Greens' lifestyle as "very gracious southern living," a manner that she felt took her back into "another era," one marked by elegance and civility. However, civility was lacking somewhat in this household due to the ongoing brother-sister feud. Jennie and Preston may have been at the same table, but they continued to refuse to speak to each other, a situation not hidden from guests. In addition, Jennie occasionally needed to assert herself, perhaps to counteract the dominating power of her three brothers. Once when Jennie expected guests for the weekend, she felt strongly that the yard should be mowed and requested that her brothers do so. They were in no hurry, however, as they typically postponed the task until the grass grew high enough to be mowed for hay. When the weekend approached without the task accomplished, Jennie gave her brothers an ultimatum, in the words of the cook: "There'll not be another meal cooked in this house until the yard's mowed!" Responding with "Awright, Sister! Awright, Sister! I'll get it done," Willis promptly saw that the yard received proper attention!

Jennie also experienced difficulty accomplishing other domestic tasks, which might have contributed to the sometimes contentious sibling relationships. For example, for two weeks twice each year the house became a flurry of activity as Jennie hired extra help and supervised a thorough housecleaning. Her brothers not only thought this exercise unnecessary but entirely too costly. They preferred the house in a more "liveable" state as opposed to the tidy and formal, aesthetically pleasing arrangement desired by their sister. Nevertheless, Jennie's practice of cleaning continued over their protests. So although theirs was gracious living, it did not represent the most civil or the happiest of families. In fact, some "insiders" considered the household a most unhappy one.[22]

Insiders, most notably the cook and housekeeper, were able to offer more candid accounts of the family because they were intimately involved in the daily lives of the Green brothers and sister. Both of these employees became almost like family, but the division between aristocrat and laborer always remained intact. These two employees were just two of many who brought their families to the Falls community and found it so satisfying that they remained for a great portion of their lifetimes. Their decision to stay was probably influenced by the amenities the Greens offered and the services provided in the village around them.

One of the Greens' amenities grew to become the center of not only the immediate community but parts of the surrounding counties as well. The general store, where purchases could range from "cornmeal to coffins," supplied its customers nearly every need, if not want. It also served as a social meeting place where locals spent a few minutes on Saturday afternoons catching up on gossip or just enjoying a short respite from the isolation of farm life. Sometimes, because not all people in the area were on mail routes, the need to pick up mail at the Falls of Rough Post Office, located in the rear of the general store until the late 1940s, might also have provided an excuse to make the trip to "town." The post office provided an additional opportunity for the Greens, who not only served as postmasters but ensured that position with their political affiliations. With Willis a registered Republican and Preston a Democrat, they were assured of control of the post office whatever the political winds.[23]

An extended reprieve from everyday farm work might

have coincided with one of the days when the Greens brought in special freight cars to receive and transport specific farm products. On Turkey Day, for example, farmers hauled their turkeys to the Falls to be shipped to market in freight cars especially equipped with stacks of coops. Wagons lined up for a hundred yards or more as farmers awaited their turns to unload. Similar activities surrounded the sale of chickens and hogs, with farmers usually driving the latter to the Falls. During harvest season wagonloads of grain were just as numerous as those of farm animals; in fact, farmers coordinated these trips to the Falls to help reduce the required waiting period.[24]

If a laborer was lucky enough to work for the Greens, he most likely lived in one of the houses they supplied for their workers and, therefore, resided in the community "proper." That community included approximately thirty-five houses located in three sections: one in the immediate vicinity of the manor house and general store; a second known as Bugger Hill, extending northward across the river into Breckinridge County; and another, Stringtown, located southeastward along the river in Grayson County. A fourth section not considered part of the community proper was Dogtown, located just at the eastern edge of the Green property. Dogtown offered the Greens some competition with its own grocery store dating to at least the 1890s.[25]

Wages for laborers were always low, but the Greens paid more than other farm employers in the surrounding area, and the other amenities they supplied made working for them a much sought-after position. Newlywed couples often appeared at the Falls in hopes of a well-paid job as well as a dwelling. Not only did the Greens provide a house (although sometimes two couples shared the four-room structure), but they also maintained them well, providing the equipment, supplies, and labor to whitewash the outside of each worker's house every spring; and paint, though only green and pink, was available upon request for the tenants' use inside the houses. In addition, the tenant houses received electricity in the 1930s when the Greens wired the "big house."[26]

Another amenity was free grazing pasture for a cow that the Greens sold their tenants, which allowed each family to have its own milk and butter. Pasture season started each year on the first day of May, when farm manager Robert Green formally announced the pastures open and available. In the 1930s the various families who owned cows each paid local children fifteen cents per week to drive them to and from the pasture each day. The numerous barns on the property and near the houses provided overnight and winter shelter for the animals.[27]

Falls of Rough was almost the perfect rural community. It provided convenient transportation by rail or river and outside communications through the telegraph, telephone, and post office. Housing was free and well maintained. Fresh country products and produce, along with the gristmill, supplied basic food commodities, while a doctor and a barber availed their services. A church and parsonage helped meet spiritual needs, a school educated the young, and a circuit court helped fulfill legal demands. And that which could not be produced on the property was available in the general store, where credit accounts were standard. In addition to all these accommodations, the caretakers truly cared about the welfare of their workers and offered wages greater than similar establishments in the region. Not surprising, then, is the fact that several families, among them names like Beard, Davis, Eskridge, Landrum, Quertermous, Surrell, Spaulding, Stone, and Woods, moved to the Falls and remained for twenty, thirty, even fifty years or more. To many, the village of Falls of Rough afforded the ideal country life. If only its future were ensured!

Chapter Twelve

Fate Seemed to Will It So

While the first two decades of the twentieth century continued to be prosperous ones for the Greens—quite possibly the most prosperous—the Great Depression of the 1930s signaled the beginning of the decline in the Greens' fortunes. Key factors included not only the economic hard times of the period but also the advanced ages of the four owners. By 1935 Willis, the eldest, was sixty-five and Robert, the youngest, was fifty-three. And because none had married, no offspring could lend youthful energy or ideas to help in managing and updating the operations; consequently, the Greens possessed little incentive to invest in improvements for the future as it held no prospect of a continuing legacy.

Although the Great Depression did not totally decimate the Greens' assets, they did lose considerable savings, particularly in the Bank of Hardinsburg. Nevertheless, Green Brothers continued to operate on a profitable basis into the 1940s, though less so than previously. Paved highways allowed the surrounding communities greater access to the goods at other locations and thereby increased competition in all aspects of the businesses. Then soon after the Louisville and Nashville Railroad received permission on 5 May 1941 to abandon the fifty-eight mile section of track between Irvington and Hartford, train service to the Falls ceased. The unavailability of rail service, as well as the depleted state of the area's timber, contributed to the sawmill's closing only weeks afterwards. The Greens sold, dismantled, and on 14 June shipped the mill out on what was perhaps the last train to depart the Falls. No longer were farmers able to bring their produce and livestock to the railhead for shipment. And because much of the Green business had in some way been connected with the railroad, profits suffered severely.[1]

The next few years rapidly brought an end to the active affairs of the businesses of the Green family at Falls of Rough. Even though these businesses were already in decline, the brothers' deaths ultimately sealed their fate. February 1943, June 1944, May 1945—and Jennie, the sister who decades earlier had relinquished her share and involvement in the Green businesses, remained the sole survivor; the viability of the Falls rested with her. She was inexperienced in financial dealings, and the deaths of her brothers were so suddenly successive that she had had no time to prepare herself for the responsibility.

Robert Green died on 4 February 1943 at age sixty of a coronary occlusion. Although his death was unexpected, some earlier indications reveal the possibility of heart problems. While on a rare vacation in 1940, he apparently suffered enough symptoms to warrant a heart tracing, but Robert continued his trip after his doctor's assurance that he had not suffered a heart attack. Only three people other than the family attended his funeral in Louisville, and Robert, the youngest brother, was buried beside his parents in the Frankfort Cemetery. The brevity of his will, which bears a 2 August 1940 date, indicates a hasty preparation, perhaps after the heart tracing (or possibly, posthumously); it left each surviving sibling one-third share of his property. This bequest gave Jennie, who had earlier given up all her inheritance, a one-ninth share of the estate, including the house and furnishings.[2]

Seventeen months after Robert's death, on 2 June 1944, Willis died of a coronary thrombosis at Kentucky Baptist Hospital in Louisville. Willis willed Jennie his interest in the house and furnishings but specified that the income from the remainder of his estate be held in trust with one half used for the benefit of each Preston and Jennie for as long as they lived. His possessions, which included land, businesses, and stocks and bonds, had a value of $344,371.47—a rather sizable sum in 1944. Willis willed any residue of his estate, upon the death of the last surviving sibling, to the Kentucky

Green mansion, circa 1920
Courtesy Mary O'Neill, Falls of Rough

Society for Crippled Children. In addition, he left a total of $68,000, likewise to be paid upon the death of the last sibling, to several relatives and employees; the most generous of these bequests was $25,000 to Agnes Beard, his long-time and highly esteemed office employee.[3]

Ironically, the last surviving family members, Preston and Jennie, had not been on speaking terms for many years. However, their awkward situation continued for only a short time because Preston was already terminally ill with prostate cancer. He died on 17 May 1945 at age sixty-seven, only eleven months after his last surviving brother. Preston, in keeping with the long-standing rift with his sister, refused to allow Jennie, who relented to seek such permission, into his room even during the last few days of his life. And Preston, unlike both Robert and Willis, did not bequeath Jennie in "fee simple" his share of the house and furnishings. Instead, he stipulated that these possessions be sold to her at the value placed upon them for estate tax assessment purposes. After making distributions to several employees, relatives, and friends, the balance of his estate, like that of his brother Willis, was available to Jennie for the rest of her life with the remainder willed to the Kentucky Society for Crippled Children.[4]

Jennie outlived her brothers by twenty years and, for the first time, did not have to live under their scrutiny or restraints. Almost immediately she began a project to completely refurbish the manor house. While her brothers had been satisfied with the braided and fiber rugs of a previous era, old but handy temporary closets made of wood frames covered with oil cloth, and an occasional dog inside, the house of the 1950s reflected a more refined, feminine touch. Jennie purchased antiques in New Orleans and New York and, in one instance, a chandelier from the island of Guadeloupe. After her redecoration the house was beautiful but appeared more a museum than the comfortable country home it had been before her brothers' deaths.[5]

With her new-found freedom Jennie also acquired new responsibilities, primarily involving the attempt to keep the remaining businesses in operation. This task proved difficult in large part because not only was she totally unprepared, but she possessed no training or even experience in their operations. Quite possibly feeling the weight of the legacy as well as the challenge of it, Jennie tried to "hold on" and continue the businesses even though they realized little profit. In 1953 the farm operation only netted $5,843.08, while the mercantile store sustained a loss of $1,663.41. At least part of this rather poor economic performance might be attributed to Jennie's unwise business decisions. Although the trust, under the auspices of Citizens Fidelity Bank of Louisville, was responsible for the Green enterprises, Trust Officer Bart Brown allowed Jennie extensive freedom in making business decisions between 1945 and 1957 when, often against the advice of experienced employees, she insisted on doing things her way.[6]

Though Jennie's lack of expertise and refusal to heed advice contributed to the businesses' lack of profit, other factors lay beyond her control. The railroad company had long since abandoned its area tracks, people in the community traded more often in the larger metropolitan markets, and farmers no longer depended upon the gristmill for their milling needs. The end was in sight and inevitable.

But Jennie was not particularly concerned about the lack of productivity at the Falls; after all, she was approaching age eighty and financially secure. The future of her beloved ancestral home farm, her real concern, presented the dilemma. To whom should she will the property? Would they care for it with the same love and attention as she had, and would they cherish the heritage of her ancestors enough to maintain the physical surroundings? What would she do with valuable family documents and possessions? To find answers to these questions, she spent much time and effort corresponding with relatives to collect information about her ancestors, developing genealogical charts, and making inquiries to historical societies concerning the distribution of the family heirlooms.

With no close relatives she first offered to will part of the property to the Episcopal Diocese of Kentucky for use as a conference camp. Later, when she learned that the denomination had integrated, she withdrew the proposal. She then offered the property to a second cousin, Stewart Scott, who declined; he was unwilling to relinquish his plans for a future in the medical field and relocate at the Falls. Eventually, Jennie located a third cousin willing to move her family from Texas. Mary Eleanor Perry McGee, a great granddaughter of John Orlando Scott, brother to Jennie Green's mother, would inherit the entire estate known as the "home farm," which consisted of approximately three thousand acres. This bequest, including thirty thousand dollars and all tangible property on the estate, designated the whole of the property to remain in the possession of Mary McGee until her death, at which time her children gain possession and ultimate authority in its management. By 2 August 1958 Jennie had concluded most of her decision-making and recorded her first will, filing a final codicil on 13 July 1959. In her will Jennie made several bequests to family, friends, and employees and designated the dispensation of various heirlooms. Her filial obligations were complete.[7]

After several bouts with illness, primarily due to her advancing age, Jennie Scott Green died just three weeks before her eighty-seventh birthday on 5 September 1965 at Breckinridge County Memorial Hospital in Hardinsburg, Kentucky. Pierson and Sons Funeral Home in Louisville was the site of her funeral, which only a few friends, relatives, and employees attended, and burial followed in the Brown and Scott family plot in the Frankfort Cemetery. Ironically, she is buried next to her brother Preston, from whom she was estranged for much of her life.

Within hours following her funeral, most of those attending met in the office of the general store at Falls of Rough to witness the reading of Jennie's will. Some suspense surrounded her decision concerning the property, as certain employees had urged Miss Jennie to favor them with the inheritance rather than Mary McGee. Just months before her death Jennie had made a trip to Louisville with the pretense or intention of changing her will. However, Mary McGee, who had brought her husband and seven children to the Falls in 1964, did indeed inherit the beloved "home farm" as stipulated in the 1958-59 will.[8]

With the passing of "Miss Jennie," an era in Kentucky's history closed. She had done her best through her last testament to ensure the preservation of at least a portion of a property that had occupied the lives of three generations of Greens. Their wisdom, toil, persistence, and sense of duty had formed it into a type of rural dynasty, but their sole survivor was unable to preserve the viability of the once-thriving businesses and, as a result, the life of its supporting village. Only her beloved manor house and its immediately surrounding grounds retained their splendor. Tenant houses stood vacant, warehouses empty, barns idle. Remnants of the farm, gristmill, and store operations continued, but briefly, under the management of the new owner. Like Miss Jennie, Mary McGee was inexperienced and unprepared for the decisions and tasks required; a lack of profit meant only debt. The business entity could not endure.

Progress had charged its price and, without a succeeding generation of direct descendants, the Green enterprises at Falls of Rough, Kentucky, would not—could not—survive. The inevitable had finally come to pass. Fate seemed to will it so.

Epilogue

oday's scene, although really of another age, is filled with evidence that Falls of Rough, Kentucky, was once a thriving community. Vestiges of a wool carding mill, gristmill, iron bridge, and in the distance a church, parsonage, and the dilapidated shells of tenant houses offer proof of the once bustling community of 250 inhabitants. Beyond and just behind the general store sits the stately ancestral home. Although somewhat faded with time and ravages of the elements, it stands as a testament to an age and to a family that put great emphasis on style and elegance—a witness to power and wealth.

A few minutes' pause at the site offers the ear a sensation not at first obvious—the distant and somewhat muffled sound of rushing water. Once perceived, the whir of the water grows ever louder, the echo of a bygone era: logs being pulled into the mill, the whine of the circular saw as it moves relentlessly again and again through logs, the creak of well-used wagons arriving to unload the products of local farms, and the scurrying of many workmen to accommodate the farmers' needs. One such farmer must have newly sawed lumber, perhaps to patch a farm building—or to construct a coffin for a recently deceased relative. Maybe another has just time to pick up the monthly supply of flour and cornmeal, ground from the stored grain of last year's crop, or to replenish commodities not provided by his farm: coffee, sugar, smoking tobacco, a piece of calico, or that rare new pair of shoes. Or more likely the bonus is just a piece of "store bought" hard candy—a luxury.

The front porch of the general store offers a panorama of the farming in progress: horses, often thirty or more, pulling farm implements in the process of cultivating thousands of acres of earth; or these many horses standing patiently eating or resting under shade trees while their sweat-soaked handlers enjoy a brief noon respite in the store. Nearby, the blacksmith bends busily repairing the shoe of a horse or a broken plow point so that all will be ready to continue the afternoon's work.

Today the "scene" is silent except for the ever-constant roar of the water as it rushes over the milldam, inspiring the echoes of ages long past. "This may not look like much today," said long-time worker for the Greens, Arlie Eskridge, in 1963, "but in the '20s and '30s this place was hummin'!"*

*Quote taken from Jim Morrissey, "Falls of Rough: Oasis of the Past," *Louisville Courier-Journal Magazine*, 27 October 1963, 10-17.

ABBREVIATIONS USED IN THE NOTES

AG   Ann Green
EBS   Elizabeth Brown Scott
ESG   Eleanor Scott Green
            (after her marriage to Lafayette Green)
GCFC   Willis and Lafayette Green Collection,
            Filson Club, Louisville, Kentucky
GCKL   Jennie Green Collection, Kentucky Library,
            Department of Library Special Collections
            Manuscripts, Western Kentucky University,
            Bowling Green, Kentucky
GFPUL   Green Farms Papers, University Archives and
            Records Center, University of Louisville,
            Louisville, Kentucky
JSG   Jennie Scott Green
LG   Lafayette Green
MCEKU   S. I. M. Major Collection,
            University Archives and Manuscripts,
             Eastern Kentucky University,
            Richmond, Kentucky
NA   National Archives, Washington, D. C.
PHC   Papers of Henry Clay, M. I. King Library,
            University of Kentucky,
            Lexington, Kentucky
PSG   Preston Scott Green
RES   Rebecca Eleanor Scott
            (before her marriage to Lafayette Green)
RSG   Robert Scott Green
RWS   Robert Wilmot Scott
WG   Willis Green
WSG   Willis [Scott] Green (Even though his name
            was simply Willis Green, I have used his
            mother's maiden name of Scott to distinguish
            him from his great uncle of the same name.)

NOTES TO PREFACE

1. I share the sentiments dealing with historical objectivity as put forth by Bertram Wyatt-Brown in his *The House of Percy.* I have invented or contrived nothing in *The Greens of Falls of Rough,* and I have made a conscious effort to separate fact from hearsay. This work is straightforward historical narrative with limited analysis and interpretation.

NOTES TO CHAPTER ONE

1. Speech of WG to Clay Club of Alexandria, D. C., 19 July [1844], PHC. Before becoming a free city in Virginia in 1846, Alexandria was part of the District of Columbia.

2. *Messmate* was used to indicate a person that ate and lived at the same boarding house; Marriage Certificate Book 1, 1787-1843, Madison County Court House, Richmond, Kentucky. Although no absolute proof identified Willis Green's mother, sufficient evidence indicates her to have been Elizabeth Stuart; "Circular of Willis Green, to His Constituents", 1 March 1841, GCKL, Series I, box 1, fol. 5; Elizabeth Short to ESG, 12 February [1878], GCKL, Series, II, box 1, fol. 6.

3. Will Book A-1, 1787-1806, Madison County Court House, Richmond, Kentucky. On some documents the amounts were figured in pounds and on others, in dollars; Will Book A-2, 1806-1813, Madison County Court House, Richmond, Kentucky.

4. Mann Butler, *A History of the Commonwealth of Kentucky* (1834; reprint ed., Berea, Kentucky: Oscar Rucker, Jr., 1969), 360; *Report of the Adjutant General of the State of Kentucky Soldiers of the War of 1812* (Frankfort, Kentucky: E. Polk Johnson, Public Printer and Binder, [1891]), 242.

5. N. S. Shaler, *Kentucky: A Pioneer Commonwealth* (Boston: Houghton, Mifflin and Company, 1885; reprint ed., New York: AMS Press, 1973), 162-163; Butler, *A History of the Commonwealth of Kentucky,* 361. Footnote at the bottom of page 361 indicates that in a letter to Governor Shelby, General Hopkins believed the villages to be only twenty miles away; Muster and Discharge rolls of the Kentucky Volunteers in the War of 1812, NA.

6. Leland Meyer, *The Life and Times of Colonel Richard M. Johnson of Kentucky* (New York: AMS Inc., 1967), 119; Isaac Shelby to Thomas H. Shelby, 6 August 1813, Isaac Shelby Papers, M. I. King Library, Lexington, Kentucky; *Report of the Adjutant General,* 179.

7. Meyer, *Johnson of Kentucky*, 121. The exact number of volunteers that marched with Governor Shelby is difficult to ascertain. Some figures are as high as four thousand. Legend indicates that Colonel Richard Johnson killed Tecumseh in this battle, although the actual event is still debated; WG to Constituents, 1 March 1841, GCKL, Series I, box 1, fol. 5. Green continued to have trouble with this knee as witnessed by a letter dated 3 November 1818 from a doctor in Philadelphia advising him to live on milk and vegetables, take a purgative every other day, lie down as much as possible, and if necessary apply caustic alkali above and below the joint. There is a discrepancy of five days between the field and staff pay rolls and the company muster rolls concerning the total number of days served. Muster Rolls, Captain Richard C. Holder's Company, 11 Regiment Kentucky Mounted Volunteer Militia, War of 1812, NA.

8. J. H. Holland to WG, 5 January 1818, GCFC, fol. 1; J. H. Holland to WG, 31 January 1818, GCKL, Series I, box 1, fol. 4; Legal Document, 25 November 1818, GCKL, Series I, box 1, fol. 1.

9. James Cooper to WG, 31 October 1818, GCKL, Series I, box 1, fol. 2a; Ibid., Unknown to WG, 29 October 1819; Unknown to WG, 31 October 1818, 22 March 1818, GCKL, Series I, box 1, fol. 1.

10. *Marriage Bonds for Shelby County, Kentucky, 1792-1830* (Chillicothe, Ohio: Elizabeth Ellsberry, [no date]), 19. Family letters and other evidence, though difficult to corroborate, indicate that Ann's sister Margaret Allen married noted Kentucky painter Matthew H. Jouett; Michael L. Cook, *Breckinridge County Kentucky Records*, vol. 3, (Kentucky Records Series, 1984), 375; Breckinridge County Deed Book G, Hardinsburg, Kentucky; Auction papers, GCKL, Series I, box 1, fol. 4. This was an auction to settle the estate of William Davidson with whom Willis, in partnership, had previously purchased the other half of this property.

11. Document used in court case filed by Willis Green to receive title to the property purchased from William Sebastian, [no date], GCFC. Sebastian had received the land in 1827 from his father Benjamin, a member of the Kentucky Court of Appeals, who had been implicated in a conspiracy to deliver Kentucky into the hands of the Spanish government. After exposure in 1806 that Sebastian had received a pension from the Spanish governor for the years 1795 to 1806, he was allowed to resign from the court. Then in 1811 he moved from Jefferson County to Grayson County, where he purchased two hundred acres, including the mill site at the falls of Rough Creek, from the heirs of Isaac Hite. He soon built a sawmill and gristmill and by 1820 was also operating a distillery at the location. Further information about Benjamin Sebastian can be found in the *Filson Club Quarterly*, "Benjamin Sebastian and the Spanish Conspiracy in Kentucky," 20 (April 1946): 107-130.

12. Papers in lawsuit brought by Willis Green in Chancery Court, Grayson County, Kentucky, [no date], GCFC.

13. Grayson County, Kentucky, tax records for 1831, Microfilm file, Kentucky Library, Bowling Green, Kentucky. Tax records indicate that the Rough Creek tract contained 220 acres.

14. Contract between Willis Green and Robert Armstrong, 29 March 1832, GCFC.

15. The store ledger indicates for the period from 13 November 1832 to 14 March 1835 that Benjamin Sebastian worked for Green on several occasions with a total credit to his account of $72.90. Who was responsible for these credits and debits is unclear because there are indications that Sebastian died in 1834. Ledger of the store and mills for 1832 through 1838. Ledger in the possession of Mary O'Neill, Falls of Rough, Kentucky.

16. Incorporation papers, [no date], GCFC; Affadavit in a lawsuit in Breckinridge County Chancery Court between Willis Green and Jefferson Jennings, [no date], GCKL, Series I, box 1, fol. 4

17. John H. Birth to Willis Green, 12 September 1836. GCKL, Series I, box 1, fol. 1. Letter contains detailed drawings for the proposed stonework for the foundation and the window headers and sills; Bill for materials from John Hardin, 11 November 1839, GCFC.

18. R. Graham to WG, 1 February 1843, GCKL, Series I, box 1, fol. 2; Unknown to WG, 12 January 1844, GCFC.

19. Unknown to WG, 23 April 1824, GCKL, Series I, box 1, fol. 1. Letter indicates Green had a slave named Ben that had run away; Receipt for slave, 5 April 1835, GCKL, Series I, box 1, fol. 4; Grayson County, Kentucky, tax records for the years 1831 to 1844, Microfilm File, Kentucky Library, Bowling Green, Kentucky. While the typical Kentucky slaveholder during the 1840s owned four or five slaves, Green generally owned twelve or thirteen, including children.

20. Affidavit filed in Breckinridge County Court, [no date], GCKL, Series I, box 1, fol. 4. References to these stores, although limited, indicate that he either owned them outright or in partnership. A *smooth face* seemed to indicate that a man was upstanding and honest; Circuit Court Orders Book 16, p. 199, Breckinridge County Court House, Hardinsburg, Kentucky.

NOTES TO CHAPTER TWO

1. W. H. Perrin, J. H. Battle, G. C. Kniffen, Kentucky: *A History of the State* (Louisville, Kentucky: F. G. Battey and Company, 1887), 312; James C. Klotter, *The Breckinridges of Kentucky, 1760-1981*

(Lexington, Kentucky: University of Kentucky Press, 1986), 47.

2. Richard H. Collins' *History of Kentucky* indicates that the winter of 1827-1828 was extremely wet; Kentucky, General Assembly, Senate, *Journal,* 3 December 1827, 223; Kentucky, General Assembly, House, *Reports,* 1836-37, 3; Kentucky, General Assembly, House, *Journal,* 1837, 4.

3. Perrin, Battle, Kniffin, *Kentucky: A History of the State,* 321.

4. Mark Hardin to Henry Clay, 5 August 1839, PHC, vol. 9, 334. The writer of the letter was apparently mistaken about the resident county of Willis Green, who was from Grayson County; George Able to Willis Green, 23 February 1840, GCKL, Series I, box 1, fol. 2; Letter of certification from the sheriffs of Hardin, Green, Hart, Meade, Breckinridge, and Grayson Counties, 19 August 1839, GCKL, Series I, box 1, fol. 5.

5. Robert V. Remini, *Henry Clay: Statesman for the Union* (New York: W. W. Norton and Company, 1991), 558.

6. Approximate duration of speech was determined by timed oral reading of text; "Speech of Mr. Green of Kentucky, on the Subtreasury Bill: Delivered in the House of Representatives, June 30, 1840", GCKL, Series I, box 1, fol. 5.

7. Ibid.; J. Gideon to WG, 21 July 1840, GCKL, Series I, box 1, fol. 4; Remini, *Henry Clay,* 558.

8. U. S., Congress, House, *Journal,* 2nd Session, 26th Congress, 7.

9. Footnote, HCP, vol. 9, 386; U. S., Congress, House, *Journal,* 2nd Session, 26th Congress, 150.

10. "Remarks of Mr. Green of Kentucky on The General Appropriations Bill. Delivered in the House of Representatives, Feb. 18, 1841", GCFC.

11. *Niles' National Register,* 20 March 1841, vol. LX, 34; Ibid. Even though Green's name is not listed, I feel reasonably certain that he was a part of this group. The article states that the paper was unable to obtain a complete list of the veterans in the parade; Freeman Cleaves, *Old Tippecanoe* (New York: Scribner's Sons, 1939), 338. General Harrison refused to wear his hat and overcoat while riding in the inaugural parade or even during his one hour and forty minute inaugural address.

12. Remarks in Senate, 9 March 1841, PHC, vol. 9, 512; Remini, *Henry Clay,* 574.

13. "Circular of Willis Green, To His Constituents," 1 March 1841, GCKL, Series I, box 1, fol. 5.

14. Henry Clay to WG, 4 May [1843], PHC, Supplement, 290.

15. Remini, *Henry Clay,* 597, 603.

16. L. G. H. McGay[?] to WG, 1 January 1841, GCKL, Series I, box 1, fol. 2.

17. *Niles' National Register*, 15 May 1841, vol. LX, 172.

18. Henry Clay to John J. Crittenden, 3 June 1842, PHC, vol. 9, 706; U. S., Congress, House, *Journal*, 2nd Session, 27th Congress, 565; *Congressional Globe*, 3rd Session, 27th Congress, 17 January 1843, 166.

19. U. S., Congress, House, Journal, 2nd Session, 27th Congress, 990. When the House of Representatives voted on 17 June 1842 to concur with the Senate in changing the new ratio from 50,179:1 (the number the House proposed) to 70,680:1 (the number the Senate proposed), the House voted to go along with the ratio set by the Senate. Green voted in the negative on this issue.

20. *Frankfort Commonwealth*, 18 April 1843, 13 June 1843.

21. *Locofoco* was believed derived from a self-lighting cigar called a locofoco. The term was first used in its political context after a group of New York Tammany Hall Democrats held a meeting by the light of candles and locofocos. This faction of the Democratic Party was generally made up of hard money men, but Whigs liberally applied the term rather derisively to all Democrats of the period.

22. *Niles' National Register*, 7 October 1843, vol. LXV, 89.

23. A bound collection of speeches used by the Whigs in Henry Clay's 1844 presidential campaign (book is in the possession of the author of this work and the title is illegible); Henry Clay to Henry White, 15 June 1844, PHC, vol. 10, 120. Whether Willis Green and Garrett Davis were the only members of this committee to hand out literature or just two members of a larger body is vague, although they appear to be the only members. In 1844, Garrett Davis was the representative from the Eighth Congressional District of Kentucky made up of the counties of Bourbon, Fayette, Jessamine, Woodford, Scott, Franklin and Owen; Ibid., Henry Clay to Cassius M. Clay, 18 September 1844, 118; Henry Clay to Benjamin W. Leigh, 30 September 1844, 128; Ibid., Henry Clay to John J. Crittenden, 21 April 1844, 47; Ibid., Henry Clay to WG, 24 August 1844, 103.

24. O. F. Mackey to WG, 2 April 1844, GCKL, Series I, box 1, fol. 6.

25. Speech of Willis Green to the Clay Club of Alexandria, D. C., 19 July [1844], HCP. The speech was apparently used as part of the campaign literature distributed throughout the nation to promote Clay's candidacy. It was commercially printed with an addendum of facts about tariff items and statements of Clay in regard to the tariff.

26. W. L. Conklin to WG, 1 April 1844, GCKL, Series I, box 1, fol. 2.

27. Howard House to WG, 11 March 1845, GCKL, Series I, box 1, fol. 2; Henry Clay to Central Committee of New York City, 25

April 1845, PHC, vol. 10, 220.

28. *Louisville Journal,* 29 April 1845; *Biographical Directory of the American Congress 1774-1927* (Washington: Government Printing Office, 1928), 1264.

29. WG to Whig Party, 25 May 1849, GCKL, Series I, box 1, fol. 3; Handwritten speech, GCKL, Series I, box 1, fol. 3.

30. Whether Napoleon ever lived for any extended period with Willis and Ann Green is not known, though a tombstone indicates he is buried only a few hundred yards from the manor house at Falls of Rough; Elizabeth Green married William T. Short of Rumsey, Kentucky. Their children were Lillie, Jennie, Willis Green, George and Joseph. Malvina Green married on 24 September 1856, Ezekial Fleming, a miller by trade, of Rumsey, Kentucky. Their children were Florence and Lafayette Green. McLean County, Kentucky Census 1870; Marriage Register A, McLean County Court House, Calhoun, Kentucky; Napoleon Green to LG, 14 March 1854, GCKL, Series II, box 3, fol. 3; Kentucky Vital Records, Grayson County Kentucky Deaths, Series 3, Vol. 43, 18.

31. WG to LG, 4 June 1860, GCKL, Series II, box 3, fol. 3.

32. ESG to EBS, 10 November 1867, MCEKU. Apparently Lafayette made a trip to Texas at or near the time of his uncle's death but did not return the body to Kentucky until 1867; Burial records, Cave Hill Cemetery, Louisville, Kentucky.

NOTES TO CHAPTER THREE

1. WG to LG, 4 June 1860, GCKL, Series II, box 3, fol. 3.

2. During the latter half of the nineteenth century, Rumsey, just across the Green River from Calhoun, county seat of McLean County, was a busy river port; WSG to Lucy Robertson, 9 May 1936, GFPUL; AG to LG, 28 March [no year], GCKL, Series II, box 3, fol. 4; WG to LG, 15 December 1854, GCKL, Series I, box 1, fol. 2.

3. Azro Dyer to LG, 9 July 1857, GCKL, Series II, box 4, fol. 5.

4. Kentucky, General Assembly, House, *Journal,* 1859, 56-61.

5. George Caldwell to LG, 16 March 1860, GCKL, Series II, box 4, fol. 5; AG to LG, 6 July [1859], GCKL, Series II, box 3, fol. 4

6. Klotter, *Breckinridges of Kentucky,* 114.

7. Horace Greeley and John F. Cleveland, compilers, *Political Textbook for 1860* (New York: Tribune Associates, 1860), 47.

8. Lewis Collins and Richard H. Collins, *Historical Sketckes of Kentucky*, vol. 1, (Covington, Kentucky, 1874; reprint, Frankfort, Kentucky: Kentucky Historical Society, 1966), 84; Greeley and Cleveland, *Political Textbook for 1860*, 48.

9. Thomas D. Clark, *Footloose in Jacksonian America* (Frankfort, Kentucky: Kentucky Historical Society, 1989), 154.

10. AG to LG, [date illegible], GCKL, Series II, box 3, fol. 4; Ibid., AG to LG, 6 July [no year].

NOTES TO CHAPTER FOUR

1. Nathanial Gaither to LG, 16 March 1860, GCKL, Series II, box 4, fol. 5; Emma Payne to LG, 4 February 1858, GCKL, Series II, box 4, fol. 5; Ibid., Anonymous to LG, 1 April 1854.

2. Although some accounts give her name as Eleanor Rebecca, convincing evidence supports the birthname Rebecca Eleanor. At the age of twelve, she signed several essays in a school composition book either "R E Scott" or "R Ella Scott," GCKL, Series II, box 1, fol. 1. In a letter responding to an inquiry of Lafayette Green to Preston B. Scott after Ella's death, Preston indicated that the family record showed "Rebecca Eleanor Scott born April 9th 1841," GCKL, Series II, box 3, fol. 5. The obituary of Robert W. Scott, contained in a scrapbook in the possession of Mary O'Neill, Falls of Rough, Kentucky, lists her name as Rebecca E.; The Green Collection at the Kentucky Library, Bowling Green, Kentucky, contains an extensive collection of material on Robert W. Scott, and the Filson Club, Louisville, Kentucky, also houses several related items, including one of Scott's farm books. The rest of the Scott material is scattered in several locations including some in the possession of the author of this work;ESG to EBS, 2 February 1867, GCKL, Series II, box 1, fol. 5.

3. LG to RES, 15 March 1865, GCKL, Series II, box 1, fol., 2a; Ibid., LG to RES, 26 May 1865; Ibid., LG to RES, 4 June 1865.

4. Ibid., LG to RES, 3 September 1865, 24 October 1865; Ibid., LG to RES, 14 February 1866.

5. Ibid., LG to RES, 10 December 1865.

6. Ibid., LG to RES, 23 December 1865; Ibid., LG to RES, 10 December 1865, 14 February 1866, 21 February 1866, 8 March 1866.

7. Ibid., LG to RES, 21 February 1866; Ibid., LG to RES, 3 September 1865; Ibid., LG to RES, 5 August 1866; LG to RWS, 13 August 1866, MCEKU.

8. LG to RES, 1 October 1866, GCKL, Series II, box 1, fol. 2a; Ibid., LG to RES, 14 February 1866; *Frankfort Tri-Weekly Yeoman,* 13 October 1866.

9. ESG to EBS, 2 February 1867, GCKL, Series II, box 1, fol. 5.

10. LG to RES, 3 September 1865, GCKL, Series II, box 1, fol. 2a; ESG to EBS, 2 February 1867, GCKL, Series II, box 1, fol. 5.

NOTES TO CHAPTER FIVE

1. School composition book of Eleanor Scott Green, GCKL, Series II, box 1, fol. 1; LG to ESG, 24 October 1865, GCKL, Series II, box 1, fol. 2a; Ibid., LG to ESG, 10 December 1865. The Frankfort and Lexington Road passed through the Locust Hill property while the Frankfort and Versailles Turnpike passed along the western boundary.

2. Ibid., LG to ESG, 3 September 1865.

3. ESG to EBS, 10 November 1867, MCEKU.

4. Ibid., ESG to EBS, 10 November 1867; ESG to EBS, 2 February 1867, GCKL, Series II, box 1, fol. 5.

5. ESG to EBS, 2 February 1867, GCKL, Series II, box 1, fol. 5; LG to ESG, 15 March 1870, GCKL, Series II, box 1, fol. 2a; ESG to EBS, 2 February 1867, GCKL, Series II, box 1, fol. 5; RWS to ESG, 30 December 1866, GCKL, Series II, box 1, fol. 4; Ibid., EBS to ESG, 1 December 1866.

6. ESG to EBS, 10 November 1867, MCEKU.

7. ESG to EBS, 2 February 1867, GCKL, Series II, box 1, fol. 5; EBS to ESG, 29 June 1872, GCKL, Series II, box 1, fol. 4; ESG to EBS, 2 February 1867, GCKL, Series II, box 1, fol. 5.

8. AG to ESG, 17 August [1868], GCKL, Series II, box 1, fol. 6; ESG to Preston Scott, 8 March 1874, GCKL, Series II, box 1, fol. 5.

9. Ibid., ESG to RWS & EBS, 18 January 1871; Ibid., ESG to RWS & EBS, 4 February 1872.

10. Ibid., ESG to Henrietta Scott, 24 April 1877.

11. ESG to RWS and EBS, 7 August 1870, GCKL, Series II, box 1, fol. 5; LG to ESG, 15 March 1870, GCKL, Series II, box 1, fol. 2b; ESG to WSG, 9 September [1887], GCKL, Series III, box 1, fol. 1; LG to ESG, 13 October 1880, GCKL, Series II, box 1, fol. 2b; ESG to RWS, 7 August 1870, GCKL, Series II, box 1, fol. 5.

12. LG to ESG, 1 January 1870, GCKL, Series II, box 1, fol. 2b; ESG to RWS, 7 August 1870, GCKL, Series II, box 1, fol. 5; Ibid., ESG to EBS & RWS, 4 February 1872.

13. Ibid., ESG to RWS & EBS, 4 March 1883.

14. Ibid., ESG to RWS & EBS, 18 January 1871.

15. LG to WSG, 23 November 1887, GCKL, Series III, box 1, fol. 2; JSG to PSG, 26 March 1896, GCKL, Series III, box 2, fol. 5; EBS

to ESG, 23 November 1883, GCKL, Series II, box 1, fol. 4; LG to JSG, 7 December 1897, GCKL, Series IV, box 1, fol. 1; ESG to JSG, 24 November 1894, GCKL, Series IV, box 1, fol. 3; ESG to WSG, [no date], GCKL, Series III, box 1, fol. 1; Jennie Short to ESG, 11 January 1875, GCKL, Series II, box 5, fol. 6.

16. ESG to EBS, 2 February 1867, GCKL, Series II, box 1, fol. 5; ESG to PSG, [no date], GCKL, Series III, box 2, fol. 5; AG to ESG, 17 August [no year], GCKL, Series II, box 1, fol. 6; ESG to WSG, 24 March 1887, GCKL, Series III, box 1, fol. 1; ESG to EBS & RWS, 4 February 1872, GCKL, Series II, box 1, fol. 5; Harriet Griswald to ESG, 18 November [no year], GCKL, Series II, box 1, fol. 7.

17. ESG to EBS, 4 March 1883, GCKL, Series II, box 1, fol. 5; Ibid., ESG to EBS, 2 February 1867.

18. LG to ESG, 29 September 1869, GCKL, Series II, box 1, fol. 2b; ESG to EBS, [no date], GCKL, Series II, box 1, fol. 5; Jane E. Scott to ESG, 7 September 1894, GCKL, Series II, box 1, fol. 4.

19. JSG to RSG, 10 October 1898, GCKL, Series III, box 2, fol. 6; AG to ESG, 17 August [no year], GCKL, Series II, box 1, fol. 6; RWS to ESG, 22 December 1875, GCKL, Series II, box 1, fol. 4; Ibid., RWS to ESG, 12 March 1884, GCKL; LG to WSG, 21 June 1888, GCKL, Series III, box 1, fol. 2; ESG to WSG, 21 September 1888, GCKL, Series III, box 1, fol. 1.

20. AG to ESG, 17 August [no year], GCKL, Series II, box 1, fol. 6; Ibid., AG to ESG, 3 August [no year]; ESG to WSG, 5 May 1886, GCKL, Series III, box 1, fol. 1; Ibid., ESG to WSG, [no date]; ESG to EBS, 2 February 1867, GCKL, Series II, box 1, fol. 5.

21. ESG to WSG, 7 May 1887, GCKL, Series III, box 1, fol. 1; ESG and EBS, [no date], GCKL, Series II, box 1, fol. 5.

22. ESG to RWS & EBS, 4 February 1872, GCKL, Series II, box 1, fol. 5; Ed Moorman to LG, 9 January 1884, GCKL, Series II, box 4, fol. 6; A. M. McCracken to LG, 16 June 1892, GCKL, Series II, box 5, fol. 9. In August 1892 the Louisville, St Louis and Texas Railroad bought out the Louisville, Hardinsburg and Western Railroad, which ran from Irvington to Fordsville with a branch line to Falls of Rough.

23. Burl St. Clair, Interview by Tom Owen, 22 August 1979, tape recording, CFPUL.

24. J. Fry Lawrence to ESG, 14 January 1893, GCKL, Series II, box 1, fol. 7; Ibid., J. Fry Lawrence to ESG, 11 January 1893.

25. Ibid.

26. ESG to EBS, 10 November 1867, MCEKU.

27. LG to ESG, 3 November 1869, GCKL, Series II, box 1, fol. 2b; ESG to WSG, 13 January 1884, GCKL, Series III, box 1, fol. 1.

28. ESG to Henrietta Scott, 24 April 1877, GCKL, Series II, box 1, fol. 5; Continental Life Insurance Co. of New York to LG, GCKL, Series II, box 4, fol. 6; Invoice from Market St. Architectural

Foundry and Iron Works, Louisville, Kentucky, 19 August 1879, GCKL, Series II, box 5, fol. 8.

29. LG to ESG, 13 October 1880, GCKL, Series II, box 1, fol. 2b; John Shillito & Co. to ESG, 20 April 1881, GCKL, Series II, box 1, fol. 7; ESG to WSG, 3 April 1887, GCKL, Series III, box 1, fol. 1.

NOTES TO CHAPTER SIX

1. AG to ESG, 29 April [no year], GCKL, Series II, box 1, fol. 6; LG to ESG, 28 April 1867, GCKL, Series II, box 1, fol 2b; RWS to LG, 5 May 1867, GCKL, Series II, box 3, fol. 5.

2. LG to ESG, 12 August 186[?], GCKL, Series II, box 1, fol. 2b; AG to ESG, 3 August 1868, GCKL, Series II, box 1, fol. 6; LG to ESG, 18 August 1868, GCKL, Series II, box 1, fol. 2b; Ibid., LG to ESG, 17 September 1868; Ibid., LG to ESG, 3 October 1868.

3. Ibid., Mary Scott Major to ESG, 2 May 1869; Ibid., Ellen Scott to ESG, 1 September 1869; Bayless E. Hardin, "Dr. Preston W. Brown 1775-1826 His Family and Descendants," *Filson Club Quarterly* (January, 1945), reprinted for Liberty Hall, Incorporated, Frankfort, Kentucky, 17; LG to ESG, 29 September 1869, GCKL, Series II, box 1, fol. 2b.

4. Louise Scott Wing to ESG, 6 October 1869, GCKL, Series II, box 1, fol. 4; Preston Scott to ESG, 14 November 1869, GCKL, Series II, box 1, fol. 1.

5. Preston Scott to LG, 4 January 1870, GCKL, Series II, box 3, fol. 5. LG to ESG, 15 March 1870, GCKL, Series II, box 1, fol. 2b.

6. ESG to RWS, 7 August 1870, GCKL, Series II, box 1, fol. 5.

7. Ibid., ESG to Queen [Mary Scott Major], 2 October 1870.

8. Ibid., ESG to RWS & EBS, 18 January 1871.

9. Ibid., ESG to RWS & EBS, 4 February 1872.

10. Ibid., ESG to Preston Scott, [no day] June 1873.

11. RSG to EBS, 20 June [1873], GCKL, Series II, box 2, fol. 1.

12. ESG to PS, 18 March 1874, GCKL, Series II, box 1, fol. 5; Preston Scott to ESG, 13 September 1874; Jane E. Scott to ESG, 15 September 1874, GCKL, Series II, box 1, fol. 4; LG to ESG, 1 November 1874, GCKL, Series II, box 1, fol. 2b.

13. Jennie Short to ESG, 11 January 1875, GCKL, Series II, box 5, fol. 6; Ann Green to ESG, 26 January [1875], GCKL, Series II, box 1, fol. 6; EBS to ESG, 27 February [no year], GCKL, Series II, box 1, fol. 4a.

14. Burial Records of Cave Hill Cemetery, Louisville, Kentucky.

15. ESG to Henrietta Scott, 24 April 1877, GCKL, Series II, box 1, fol. 5. *Prizing* was the process of pressing tobacco into large casks prior to shipment to market.

16. Ibid.

17. Jennie Short to ESG, 28 April 1878, GCKL, Series II, box 1, fol. 6.

18. ESG to RWS & EBS, 4 March 1883, GCKL, Series II, box 1, fol. 5.

19. LG to ESG, 13 October 1880, GCKL, Series II, box 1, fol. 2b.

20. Burl St. Clair interview.

21. WSG to RWS & Henrietta Scott, 21 September 1881, GCKL, Series II, box 2, fol. 1.

22. Mary Scott Major to ESG, 28 September 1881, GCKL, Series II, box 1, fol. 4a; EBS to ESG, 21 June 1882, GCKL, Series II, box 1, fol. 4.

23. Mary Scott Major to ESG, 28 September 1881, GCKL, Series II, box 1, fol. 4a.

24. Genealogies of the Scott, Brown, and Wilmot families by an unknown family member. Ella Scott Green's brother, John Orlando Scott, also had a son named Robert Wilmot, born in 1869.

25. ESG to WSG, 21 November 1883, GCKL, Series III, box 1, fol. 1.

26. Ibid., ESG to WSG, 3 April 1886; Ibid., ESG to WSG, [no day] March 1886.

27. Ibid., ESG to WSG, [no day or month] 1885; Ibid., ESG to WSG, 15 January 1888.

28. M. E. Thomas to ESG, [no day] September 1891, GCKL, Series II, box 1, fol. 7; ESG to RWS & EBS, 4 March 1883, GCKL, Series II, box 1, fol. 5.

29. Jane E. Scott to ESG, 6 July [no year], GCKL, Series II, box 1, fol. 4; JSG & PSG to WSG, 21 May 1888, GCKL, Series III, box 1, fol. 4.

30. ESG to WSG, 31 [no month] 1882, GCKL, Series III, box 1, fol. 1; ESG to EBS, [no date], GCKL, Series II, box 1, fol. 5; ESG to WSG, [no day or month] 1887, GCKL, Series III, box 1, fol. 1.

31. ESG to WSG, [18] October 1887, GCKL, Series III, box 1, fol. 1; Ibid., ESG to WSG, [no date]; Ibid., ESG to WSG, [12] October 1887.

32. Ibid., ESG to WSG, 23 January 1887; Ibid., ESG to WSG, [no day or month] 1887; Ibid., ESG to WSG, [no day or month] 1885.

33. ESG to JSG, [no date], GCKL, Series IV, box 1, fol. 3.

34. Angie B. Clark to ESG, [no day] September 1888, GCKL, Series II, box 1, fol. 7; ESG to EBS, 26 August 1883, GCKL, Series II,

box 1, fol. 5; Loulie M. Leboot to ESG, 26 February [1896], GCKL, Series II, box 1, fol. 7.

35. Ibid., Mattie Graham Murray to ESG, 7 March 1896; Ibid., Rosa Todd to ESG, 29 April 1895; Ibid., Caroline Ryan to ESG, [no date].

NOTES TO CHAPTER SEVEN

1. ESG to WSG, 21 November 1883, GCKL, Series III, box 1, fol. 1.

2. JSG to LG & ESG, [25] October 1894, GCKL, Series II, box 1, fol. 3b; ESG to WSG, 9 September 1887, GCKL, Series III, box 1, fol. 1; PSG to JSG, 16 February 1896, GCKL, Series IV, box 1, fol. 5.

3. J. Fry Lawrence to ESG, 11 January 1893, GCKL, Series II, box 1, fol. 7; EBS to RWS, 20 June [no year], Henrietta Mitchell Wiley Collection, Liberty Hall, Frankfort, Kentucky; ESG to WSG, 7 May 1887, GCKL, Series III, box 1, fol. 1; Charles Armstrong to ESG, 20 November 1894, GCKL, Series II, box 1, fol. 7.

4. *Breckinridge County News* (Hardinsburg, Kentucky), 30 August 1893, GFPUL.

5. *Breckinridge County News*, 26 July 1893.

6. J. Fry Lawrence to ESG, [no day] September [1893], GCKL, Series II, box 1, fol. 7.

7. Jane E. Scott to ESG, 15 September [no year], GCKL, Series II, box 1, fol. 4.

8. ESG to WSG, 23 January 1887, GCKL, Series III, box 1, fol. 1; LG to WSG, 25 March 1888, GCKL, Series III, box 1, fol. 2; ESG to WSG, [no day] April 1891, GCKL, Series III, box 1, fol. 1.

NOTES TO CHAPTER EIGHT

1. AG to ESG, 26 January [no year], GCKL, Series II, box 1, fol. 6. *Flux* was a term used to identify a discharge from the body, as in dysentery; ESG to EBS, 26 August [1883], GCKL, Series II, box 1, fol. 5; ESG to WSG, [no date], GCKL, Series III, box 1, fol. 1; Ibid., ESG to WSG, 9 September [1887]; Ibid., ESG to WSG, [no date]; J. Fry Lawrence to ESG, 14 January 1893, GCKL, Series II, box 1, fol. 7; ESG to Preston Scott, [no day] June 1873, GCKL, Series II, box 1, fol. 5.

2. Ibid.; AG to ESG, 17 August [no year], GCKL, Series II, box 1, fol. 6.

3. ESG to EBS, [no date], GCKL, Series II, box 1, fol. 5; Ibid., ESG to Queen [Mary Scott Major], 2 October 1870.

4. ESG to WSG, 11 May 1888, GCKL, Series III, box 1, fol. 1; ESG to EBS, 2 February 1867, GCKL, Series II, box 1, fol. 5; Ibid., ESG to EBS & RWS, 18 January 1871; Ibid., ESG to EBS & RWS, 4 February 1872; ESG to JSG, 24 November 1894, GCKL, Series IV, box 1, fol. 3; LG to ESG, [no date], GCKL, Series II, box 1, fol. 2b; ESG to WSG, 27 March 1884, GCKL, Series III, box 1, fol. 1

5. LG to ESG, [no date], GCKL, Series II, box 1, fol. 2b; ESG to WSG, [no date], GCKL, Series III, box 1, fol. 1; Ibid., ESG to WSG, 5 May 1886. Calomel was generally used as a purgative.

6. ESG to EBS, 2 February 1867, GCKL, Series II, box 1, fol. 5; ESG to WSG, 5 May 1886, GCKL, Series III, box 1 fol. 1; F. B. Staines to LG, 5 March 1891, GCKL, Series II, box 4, fol. 9; ESG to JSG, 18 November 1895, GCKL, Series IV, box 1, fol. 3.

·7. ESG to EBS, [no date], GCKL, Series II, box 1, fol. 5; Delegate's card, 13 August 1895, GCKL, Series II, box 1, fol. 7; ESG to PSG, 6 December 1895, GCKL, Series II, box 1, fol. 5.

8. *Owensboro Daily Messenger*, 28 February 1896, 11 March 1896; *Louisville Courier-Journal*, 10 March 1896.

9. Rumsey Scott to Jane E. Scott, 1 March 1896, GCKL, Series II, box 2, fol. 1.

NOTES TO CHAPTER NINE

1. LG to ERS, 8 March 1866, GCKL, Series II, box 1, fol. 2a.

2. RWS to EG, 9 January 1868, GCKL, Series II, box 1, fol. 4; Ibid., RWS to LG, 9 January 1869.

3. Gatewood and Thomas, Atts. to LG, 26 January 1880, GCKL, Series II, box 4, fol. 6; LG to JSG, 30 October 1896, GCKL, Series IV, box 1, fol. 2; RSG to LG, 26 April 1899, GCKL, Series II, box 3, fol. 2.

4. A *freshet* described an amount of rainfall required to cause a small rise in the river level.

5. ESG to WSG, [no date], GCKL, Series III, box, 1, fol. 1; LG to WSG, 1 April 1888, GCKL, Series III, box 1, fol. 2. A hotel containing several rooms was located approximately one hundred yards down river from the gristmill. The hotel was destroyed by fire in June 1909.

6. WSG to Lucy K. Robertson, 9 May 1936, GFPUL; JSG to

RSG, 9 February 1900, GCKL, Series III, box 2, fol. 6.

    7. ESG to WSG, [no day or month] 1887, GCKL, Series III, box 1, fol. 1; R. Graham to WG, 1 February 1843, GCKL, Series II, box 1, fol. 2; LG to WSG, 23 November 1887, GCKL, Series III, box 1, fol. 2. Evidence suggests that from at least sometime in the 1840s the mills at Falls of Rough were powered by turbine wheels rather than overshot or undershot wheels. If this was true, then the use of these wheels was very technologically innovative for the period; RWS to LG, 26 November 1866, GCKL, Series II, box 3, fol. 5; RWS to LG, 11 March 1883, GCKL, Series II, box 3, fol. 6; J. C. Percefull to LG, 29 August 1887, GCKL, Series II, box 4, fol. 8; T. F. Nichols to LG, 13 August 1888, GCKL, Series II, box 4, fol. 8. The stone dam backed up the headwater for the mills until 1968 and is still standing today.

    8. Maury Klein, *History of the Louisville and Nashville Railroad* (New York: McMillian Co., 1972), 138; Elmer G. Sulzer, *Ghost Railroads of Kentucky* (Indianapolis, Indiana: Van Jones and Company, [no date]), 138; George Triplett to LG, 3 August 1888, GCKL, Series III, box 2, fol. 6. Evidence indicates that Lafayette was a stockholder in the Owensboro, Falls of Rough and Green River Railroad Company.

    9. Lee A. Dew, "The Fordsville Road: The Building of the Owensboro, Falls of Rough and Green River Railroad," *Daviess County Historical Society Quarterly* (April 1986): 28; Frank Peyton to WSG, 20 February 1889, GCKL, Series III, box 1, fol. 2.

    10. Ibid., LG to WSG, 10 June 1888. Lafayette casually referred to the proposed company as the Irvington, Hardinsburg and Falls of Rough Railroad, instead of the official name of the chartered company. Perhaps his reference was the first intended name of the new railroad; Unknown to WSG, 5 December 1889, GCKL, Series III, box 1, fol. 6; Sulzer, *Ghost Railroads*, 133; George H. Lamkin to LG, 1 September 1892, GCKL, Series II, box 5, fol. 1; Sulzer, *Ghost Railroads*, 135.

    11. WSG to JSG, 1 November 1895, GCKL, Series IV, box 1, fol. 4; J. Fry Lawrence to LG, 23 March 1893, GCKL, Series II, box 5, fol. 2; ESG to JSG, 20 April 1895, GCKL, Series IV, box 1, fol. 3.

    12. WSG to JSG, [no day or month] 1895, GCKL, Series IV, box 1, fol. 4.

    13. *Breckinridge County News*, 16 January 1907; ESG to WSG, 5 May 1886, GCKL, Series III, box 1, fol. 1.

    14. William E. Stone to LG, 6 May 1892, GCKL, Series II, box 5, fol. 9.

    15. Certification of vote totals by Breckinridge County Court Clerk, 4 August 1881, GCKL, Series II, box 5, fol. 7; Edward O. Brown, Clerk of Grayson County to LG, GCKL, Series II, box 4, fol. 6; Kentucky, General Assembly, Senate, *Journal*, 1881-1882, 44, 623.

16. Telegram, 28 January 1907. Telegram is in possession of
Mary O'Neill, Falls of Rough, Kentucky; Unidentified newspaper clip-
ping, Green Family, Kentucky Room Vertical File, Owensboro Public
Library, Owensboro, Kentucky.

17. Thomas T. Crittenden to WSG, 30 January 1907, GCKL,
Series III, box 2, fol. 2. Crittenden was a former resident of Breckinridge
County, Kentucky, and governor of Missouri from 1880 to 1884.

18. *R. L. Polk & Company's Kentucky State Gazetteer and
Business Directory for 1895-96,* (reprint ed., Utica, Kentucky: McDowell
Publishing Company, 1985), 82.

NOTES TO CHAPTER TEN

1. ESG to WSG, [no day] March 1886, GCKL, Series III, box
1, fol. 1. Rev. William Lewis Breckinridge was president of Centre
College in the early 1860s, and his older brother Robert John
Breckinridge was a professor at Princeton Theological Seminary at
Princeton, New Jersey, in the late 1830s. The Breckinridges and Scotts
are related through the descendants of John Preston and Elizabeth
Patton. *The Breckinridges of Kentucky* by James C. Klotter is an excellent
account of the more famous members of the Breckinridge family; Clark,
Footloose in Jacksonian America, 160.

2. WSG to RWS, 13 November 1883, GCKL, Series II, box 2,
fol. 1. The Institute occupied several locations over the years, including
Franklin Springs, Farmdale, and Lyndon, Kentucky. In 1883 tuition was
$300 and included washing, fuel, lights, and rent of furnished room for
forty weeks.

3. Robert D. Allen to LG, 22 October 1883, GCKL, Series II,
box 4, fol. 4; WSG to RWS, 4 March 1884, GCKL, Series II, box 2, fol.
1; ESG to WSG, 26 April 1884, GCKL, Series II, box 1, fol. 1;
Catalogue of the Kentucky Military Institute for the year ending 6 June
1885, Kentucky Historical Society, Frankfort, Kentucky. Willis Green's
Kentucky Military Institute uniform remains in the possession of Mary
O'Neill at Falls of Rough, Kentucky.

4. W. G. Turnall to WSG, 18 November 1882, GCKL, Series
III, box 1, fol. 5; ESG to WSG, 3 May 1888, 2 June 1886, 10 February
1889, GCKL, Series III, box 1, fol. 1.

5. WSG to ESG, 2 November [1887], GCKL, Series II, box 1,
fol. 3a; R. J. Owen to WSG, 11 April 1886, GCKL, Series III, box 1,
fol. 5; Ibid., Unknown to WSG, 6 November 1886; Dwight N. Marble
to WSG, 24 April 1887, GCKL, Series III, box 1, fol. 5.

6. Ibid., W. G. Hall to WSG, 31 April 1887.

7. Unknown to WSG, 20 June 1892, GCKL, Series III, box 1,

fol. 6; Julia Lawrence to WSG, 10 January 1890, GCKL, Series III, box 2, fol. 1; Isabelle McHenry to WSG, 14 December 1882, GCKL, Series III, box 2, fol. 2; W. G. Hall to WSG, 5 January 1890, GCKL, Series III, box 2, fol. 1.

8. ESG to WSG, 13 January 1884, GCKL, Series III, box 1, fol. 1; Ibid., ESG to WSG, 21 September 1887; J. W. Cook to WSG, 4 June 1888, GCKL, Series III, box 1, fol. 6; Unknown to LG, 25 July 1881, GCKL, Series II, box 3, fol. 3; WSG to RWS, 13 November 1883, GCKL, Series II, box 2, fol. 1.

9. LG to WSG, 18 September 1886, 16 December 1886, 2 June 1887, 4 October 1887, 23 November 1887, 15 December 1887, 11 April 1889, GCKL, Series III, box 1, fol. 2.

10. Oration given by WSG, 21 June 1888, GCKL, Series III, box 1, fol. 4. Apparently classmates evaluated speeches on cards later returned to the speakers; Ibid., Oration given by WSG, 20 June 1889.

11. Minutes of the Centre College Board of Directors, 19 June 1889, Centre College, Danville, Kentucky; LG & ESG to WSG, [24] June 1889, GCKL, Series III, box 1, fol. 2.

12. WSG to JSG, 10 September 1894, GCKL, Series IV, box 1, fol. 4; LG to JSG, 24 February 1895, GCKL, Series IV, box 1, fol. 2. Samuel Ire Monger Major, Jr. (generally called Sam by family) was the son of Samuel Ire Monger Major and Mary Scott Major of Frankfort.

13. PSG to Family, 19 February 1896, GCKL, Series II, box 1, fol. 3.

14. The speculation that such behavior may have been at least partiallly responsible for the eventual split between Preston and his sister, although unsubstantiated, warrants at least some consideration; Class Record Book, vol. 3, 1882-1898, Centre College, Danville, Kentucky; *The Eccentric* (Centre College newspaper), 1897, Danville, Kentucky.

15. The Western to LG, 13 August 1890, GCKL, Series II, box 4, fol. 9; ESG to JSG, 3 September 1894, GCKL, Series IV, box 1, fol. 3. Princeton Collegiate Institute, established in 1860 and reorganized in 1881, was affiliated with the Presbyterian denomination and offered courses of study at the primary, secondary, and college levels. The first president was Rev. Heman H. Allen, a graduate of Centre College and Danville Theological Seminary.

16. Mary G. Lawrence to ESG, 9 November 1894, GCKL, Series II, box 1, fol. 6; JSG to LG & ESG, [25] October 1894, GCKL, Series II, box 1, fol. 3c.

17. Ibid.; JSG to LG, [9 January 1896], GCKL, Series II, box 3, fol. 2; ESG to JSG, 22 January 1895, GCKL, Series IV, box, 1, fol. 3; Ibid., ESG to JSG, 20 April 1895.

18. WSG to JSG, 10 September 1894, [no day or month] 1895, GCKL, Series IV, box 1, fol. 4.

19. Mary G. Lawrence to ESG, 9 November 1894, GCKL, Series II, box 1, fol. 6; Ibid., Mary G. Lawrence to ESG, 22 September 1894.

20. Shell Smith to JSG, 15 November 1894, GCKL, Series IV, box 9, fol. 1. Shelley Ransford Smith was the son of Nancy Bond Kevil Smith and John Parker Smith, a banker and prominent citizen of Princeton. Shell became a lawyer and later president of the Farmers National Bank of Princeton, Kentucky; Ibid., Shell Smith to JSG, 11 February 1898, 15 March 1898, 28 June 1898, 19 October 1898, 24 September 1933.

21. JSG to LG, [no date], GCKL, Series II, box 3, fol. 2.

22. Eleanor F. Allen to ESG, 28 February 1896, GCKL, Series II, box 1, fol. 7.

23. JSG to RSG, 27 November 1896, 29 March 1897, GCKL, Series II, box 1, fol. 6; JSG to RSG, 10 May 1900, GCKL, Series III, box, 2, fol. 6; Class Record Book, vol. 3, 1882-1898, Centre College, Danville, Kentucky; Inscribed fraternity pin is in the possession of Mary O'Neill, Falls of Rough, Kentucky.

NOTES TO CHAPTER ELEVEN

1. St. Clair interview; Carl Sarver, Falls of Rough, Kentucky, Interview by author, 6 March 1995; St. Clair interview.

2. Minutes of the yearly meeting of the Board of Directors, Rough River Bank; Bank register for 1911. Books are in the possession of Mary O'Neill, Falls of Rough, Kentucky.

3. Agnes Beard, Interview by Tom Owen, 27 June 1979, tape recording, GFPUL.

4. Murray Tate, Falls of Rough, Kentucky, Interview by author, 16 May 1995; St. Clair interview; Sarver interview.

5. Gwyn Spaulding, Interview by Tom Owen, 22 August 1979, tape recording, GFPUL.

6. St. Clair interview; Beard interview.

7. Spaulding interview.

8. Martha Brown, Interview by Tom Owen, 1979, tape recordings GFPUL; JSG to Stewart's Dry Goods Company, 28 February 1961, GCKL, Series IV, box 1, fol. 1b; Unidentified newspaper clipping, [no date], GFPUL.

9. Russell James, Hardinsburg, Kentucky, Interview by author 16 December 1995.

10. Beard interview; Brochure from Seventy-fifth Annual Session of Lily Dale Assembly, Lily Dale, New York, July 1954. Brochure is in the possession of the author of this work.

11. Beard interview; Note in Jennie Green's handwriting, 7 March 1943. Note is in the possession of the author of this work.

12. Beard interview; Astrological Forecast, GFPUL. Jennie's personal papers included this booklet of astrological analyses.

13. Deed of conveyance, 19 September 1911. Deed is in the possession of the author of this work.

14. ESG to WSG, [no date], GCKL, Series III, box 1, fol. 1.

15. *Breckinridge County News,* 16 August 1933, GFPUL.

16. Unidentified newspaper clipping is in possession of Mary O'Neill, Falls of Rough, Kentucky.

17. Brown interview.

18. Passport, 10 July 1923, GCKL, Series III, box 2, fol. 2. Passport contains the port of entry stamps for Japan and China; WSG to Florence [Flemming] and Elizabeth [Short], 2 September 1923, Ibid.; WSG to JSG, 28 May 1929, 20 June 1929, 25 June 1929, GCKL, Series IV, box 1, fol. 4.

19. Beard interview.

20. RSG to JSG, [no day] July 1903, GCKL, Series IV, box 1, fol. 5.

21. Spaulding interview; Beard interview.

22. Spaulding interview.

23. Brown interview; Tate interview.

24. St. Clair interview; Spaulding interview.

25. St. Clair interview; ESG to Jane E. Scott, 27 October 1895, GCKL, Series II, box 1, fol. 5.

26. Spaulding interview; Maydee Crawford and Pauline Beachum, McQuady, Kentucky, Interview by author, 25 January 1996; Spaulding interview.

27. Spaulding interview.

NOTES TO CHAPTER TWELVE

1. Beard interview; Frank G. Tatnall, "Fifty Years at Hardinsburg," *National Railway Bulletin* 56 (1991): 16; St. Clair interview.

2. Kentucky Death Certificate, Microfiche File, Kentucky Historical Society, Frankfort, Kentucky; H. V. Holland, MD. to Robert Green, 14 February 1940, GCKL, Series III, box 2, fol. 6; Eleanor Nugent, Owensboro, Kentucky, Interview by author, 9 July 1995; Will of Robert Scott Green, Will Book B, 341, Grayson County Court House, Leitchfield, Kentucky.

3. Kentucky Death Certificate, Microfiche File, Kentucky Historical Society, Frankfort, Kentucky; Will Book B, 389, Grayson County Court House, Leitchfield, Kentucky.

4. Kentucky Death Certificate, Microfiche File, Kentucky Historical Society, Frankfort, Kentucky.

5. Beard interview; Spaulding interview.

6. Profit and loss statements of the farm and store for 1953. These documents are in the possession of the author of this work; St. Clair interview.

7. *Louisville Courier-Journal,* 22 April 1953; Mary McGee is now Mary O'Neill.

8. Mary O'Neill, Falls of Rough, Kentucky, Interview by author, 6 March 1995; Beard interview.

Bibliography

Archival Collections

The research for this work utilized numerous sources, particularly the many pieces of personal correspondence preserved by the three generations of the Green family. The most important and extensive compilation of this material is the Jennie Green Collection housed in the Kentucky Library on the campus of Western Kentucky University, Bowling Green, Kentucky. Its 7,719 items span the years 1814 to 1965 and range from personal family letters and business correspondence to the ledgers of the several businesses owned by the Greens. The collection also contains many pieces of personal correspondence to the family of Robert Wilmot Scott of Franklin County. All material has been meticulously catalogued and is extremely easy to access. Because this collection figures so significantly in the research, I include in the notes the series, box, and folder numbers, when appropriate, as a service to the reader.

The Willis Green Papers at the Filson Club, Louisville, Kentucky, is a smaller collection containing primarily the papers of Willis Green from the period 1821 to 1859. Included in the material are political papers, land acquisition documents, and personal letters.

The Manuscripts and Archives Department of the University of Louisville Library, Louisville, Kentucky, contains in the Green Farms Papers a large collection of Green family photographs, including the family of Robert Wilmot Scott. Unfortunately, most of the photographs are unidentified and, therefore, of limited use. Also included are several of the ledgers of the Green businesses at Falls of Rough as well as interviews with employees of the Green family and local citizens who were their contemporaries.

The Archives and Manuscripts Library at Eastern Kentucky University, Richmond, Kentucky, houses the S. I. M. Major Collection. It is comprised primarily of personal letters between members of the Robert W. Scott family.

A small portion of the material used in this research is still in the possession of Mary O'Neill, present owner of the Green property. These records include business ledgers, family correspondence, photographs and paintings, and memorabilia. The author of this work is also in possession of some of the items used.

Government Publications

Kentucky. General Assembly. House. *Journal.* 1837.

Kentucky. General Assembly. House. *Reports.* 1836-1837.

Kentucky. General Assembly. Senate. *Journal.* 1827.

U. S. Congress. House. *Journal.* 27th Congress, 2nd Sess. 1841.

Public Records

Circuit Court Order Book 16, Breckinridge County Court House, Hardinsburg, Kentucky.

Deed Book G, Breckinridge County Court House, Hardinsburg, Kentucky.

Marriage Certificate Book 1, 1787-1843, Madison County Court House, Richmond, Kentucky.

Will Book A-1, 1787-1806, Madison County Court House, Richmond, Kentucky.

Will Book A-2, 1806-1813, Madison County Court House, Richmond, Kentucky.

Will Book B, Grayson County Court House, Leitchfield, Kentucky.

Institutional Records

Class Record Book, vol 3, 1882-1898, Centre College, Danville, Kentucky.

Minutes of the Centre College Board of Directors, Centre College, Danville, Kentucky.

Newspapers

Breckinridge County News, 1893.
The Eccentric, (Centre College) 1897.
Frankfort Commonwealth, 1843.
Frankfort Tri-Weekly Yeoman, 1866.
Louisville Courier-Journal, 1896, 1953.
Louisville Journal, 1845.
Niles' National Register, 1841-1843.
Owensboro Daily Messenger, 1896.

Books

Butler, Mann. *A History of the Commonwealth of Kentucky.* 1834; reprint ed., Berea, Kentucky: Oscar Rucker, Jr., 1969.

Clark, Thomas D. *Footloose in Jacksonian America.* Frankfort, Kentucky: Kentucky Historical Society, 1989.

Cleaves, Freeman. *Old Tippecanoe.* New York: Scribner and Sons, 1939.

Collins, Lewis and Richard H. Collins. *History of Kentucky.* 2 vols. Covington, Kentucky, 1874; reprint, Frankfort, Kentucky: Kentucky Historical Society, 1966.

Cook, Michael. Breckinridge County Kentucky Records. 3 vols. Kentucky Records Series, 1984.

Ellsberry, Elizabeth. *Marriage Bonds for Shelby County, Kentucky 1792-1830.* Chillicothe, Ohio: By the Author, [no date].

Greeley, Horace, and John Cleveland, compilers. *Political Textbook for 1860.* New York: Tribune Associates, 1860.

Hopkins, James F., ed. vols. 1-5; Mary W. M. Hargreaves, ed. vol. 6; Robert Seager II, ed. vols. 7-9; Melba Porter Hay, ed. vol. 10. Papers of Henry Clay. Lexington, Kentucky: University of Kentucky Press, 1959–.

Klein, Maury. *History of the Louisville and Nashville Railroad.* New York: Macmillan and Company, 1972.

Klotter, James. *The Breckinridges of Kentucky, 1768-1981.* Lexington, Kentucky: University of Kentucky Press, 1986.

Meyer, Leland. *The Life and Times of Colonel Richard M. Johnson.* New York: AMS Inc., 1967.

Perrin, W. H., J. H. Battle, and G. C. Kniffen. *Kentucky: A History of the State.* Louisville: F. G. Battey and Company, 1887.

Remini, Robert. *Henry Clay: Statesman for the Union.* New York: W. W. Norton & Company, 1991.

Report of the Adjutant General of the State of Kentucky. Frankfort, Kentucky: E. Polk Johnson, Public Printer and Binder, [1891].

Shaler, N. S. *Kentucky: A Pioneer Commonwealth.* Boston: Houghton, Mifflin and Company, 1885; reprint ed., New York: AMS Press, 1973.

Sulzer, Elmer G. *Ghost Railroads of Kentucky.* Indianapolis: Van Jones and Company [no date].

Directories and Gazetteers

Biographical Directory of the American Congress, 1774-1927. Washinton, D. C., 1928.

Polk, R. L. *Kentucky State Gazetteer and Business Directory for 1895-96.* reprint ed., Utica, Kentucky: McDowell Publishing Company, 1985.

Periodicals

Dew, Lee A. "The Fordsville Road: The Building of the Owensboro, Falls of Rough and Green River Railroad." *Daviess County Historical Society Quarterly* (April 1986): 26-36.

Hardin, Bayless E. "Dr. Preston W. Brown 1775-1826, His Family and Descendants." *Filson Club Quarterly* (January 1945), article reprinted for Liberty Hall Inc., Frankfort, Kentucky.

Tatnall, Frank G. "Fifty Years at Hardinsburg." *National Railway Bulletin* 56 (1991): 12-21.

Interviews

Beard, Agnes, Louisville, Kentucky. Interview by Tom Owen, 22 June 1979. Tape recording, Green Farms Papers, University Archives and Records Center, University of Louisville, Louisville, Kentucky.

Brown, Martha, Louisville, Kentucky. Interview by Tom Owen, 1979. Tape recording, Green Farms Papers, University Archives and Records Center, University of Louisville, Louisville, Kentucky.

Crawford, Maydee, and Pauline Beachum, McQuady, Kentucky. Interview by author, 25 January 1996.

James, Russell, Hardinsburg, Kentucky. Interview by author, 16 December 1995.

O'Neill, Mary, Falls of Rough, Kentucky. Interview by author, 6 March 1995.

Sarver, Carl, Falls of Rough, Kentucky. Interview by author, 6 March 1995.

Spaulding, Gwyn, Falls of Rough, Kentucky. Interview by Tom Owen, 22 August 1979. Tape recording, Green Farms Papers, University Archives and Records Center, University of Louisville, Louisville, Kentucky.

St. Clair, Burl, Falls of Rough, Kentucky. Interview by Tom Owen, 22 August 1979. Green Farms Papers, University Archives and Records Center, University of Louisville, Louisville, Kentucky.

Tate, Murray, Falls of Rough, Kentucky. Interview by author, 16 May 1995.

Index